Hello! 175 Dill Recipes

(Dill Recipes - Volume 1)

Best Dill Cookbook Ever For Beginners

Ms. Ingredient

Copyright: Published in the United States by Ms. Ingredient/ © MS. INGREDIENT

Published on October, 29 2019

All rights reserved. No part of this publication may be reproduced, stored in retrieval system, copied in any form or by any means, electronic, mechanical, photocopying, recording or otherwise transmitted without written permission from the publisher. Please do not participate in or encourage piracy of this material in any way. You must not circulate this book in any format. MS. INGREDIENT does not control or direct users' actions and is not responsible for the information or content shared, harm and/or actions of the book readers.

In accordance with the U.S. Copyright Act of 1976, the scanning, uploading and electronic sharing of any part of this book without the permission of the publisher constitute unlawful piracy and theft of the author's intellectual property. If you would like to use material from the book (other than just simply for reviewing the book), prior permission must be obtained by contacting the author at msingredient@mrandmscooking.com

Thank you for your support of the author's rights.

Content

- CONTENT 3
- INTRODUCTION 6
- LIST OF ABBREVIATIONS 8
- 175 AMAZING DILL RECIPES 9
  1. 'i Hate Cucumbers!' Cucumber Salad 9
  2. 20-minute Skillet Salmon 9
  3. A Lot More Than Plain Spinach Pie (greek Batsaria) 10
  4. Afghan Tomato Soup (aush Goshti) 10
  5. Angie's Dilly Casserole Bread 11
  6. Arakas Latheros (greek Peas With Tomato And Dill) 12
  7. Artichokes With Lemon & Dill 12
  8. Australian Potato Salad 13
  9. Baba's Best Sorrel Soup 13
  10. Baby Carrots With Dill Butter 14
  11. Baked Halibut Sitka 14
  12. Barney's King Salmon Gravlax 15
  13. Beef Pirozhki 15
  14. Best Buckwheat Salad 16
  15. Best-ever Cucumber Dill Salad 17
  16. Big Ray's Paleo Roasted Cauliflower 17
  17. Brown Butter & Dill Brussels Sprouts . 18
  18. Cabbage Veggie Cream Soup 18
  19. Carrot Dill Soup 19
  20. Chanterelle Mushroom And Wild Rice Soup 19
  21. Chateaubriand Con Vino Brodo 20
  22. Cheese Torte With Chicken And Mushroom 20
  23. Chef Bevski's Greek Salad 21
  24. Chicken Dilly 22
  25. Chicken With Sugar Snap Peas & Spring Herbs 22
  26. Chickpea "tuna" Salad Sandwiches 23
  27. Chilled Cucumber Yogurt Soup 23
  28. Chilled Yellow Squash Soup With Dill . 24
  29. Chilly Dilly Cucumber Soup 24
  30. Chive And Dill Muffins 25
  31. Chorizo Chicken Roll 26
  32. Classic Crab And Shrimp Salad 26
  33. Cool And Creamy Cucumber Salad 27
  34. Corn, Zucchini, And Tomato Pie 27
  35. Creamy Dill Dip 28
  36. Creamy Dill Dip Ii 28
  37. Creamy Dill Dipping Sauce 28
  38. Creamy Dill Sauce 29
  39. Creamy Herb Dip 29
  40. Crispy Cucumbers And Tomatoes In Dill Dressing 30
  41. Crispy Tofu And Bacon Wraps 30
  42. Crispy Zucchini Fritters 31
  43. Cucamelon Pickles 31
  44. Cucumber And Dill Finger Sandwiches 32
  45. Cucumber And Dill Pasta Salad 32
  46. Cucumber Slices With Dill 33
  47. Danish Meatballs With Dill Sauce 33
  48. Deep Fried Dill Pickles 34
  49. Deviled Eggs With A Dill Twist 34
  50. Dill And Shrimp Salad 35
  51. Dill Butter 35
  52. Dill Cucumber Salad 35
  53. Dill Dip Iii 36
  54. Dill Gazpacho 36
  55. Dill Pickle Dip 36
  56. Dill Pickle Sandwich Slices 37
  57. Dill Poached Salmon 37
  58. Dill Sauce For Hamburgers 38
  59. Dill Sweet Potato Fries With Vegan Dip 38
  60. Dill, Feta And Garlic Cream Cheese Spread 39
  61. Dill-infused Deviled Eggs With Bacon Crumble 39
  62. Dill-tarragon Salmon 39
  63. Dilled Creamed Potatoes 40
  64. Dilled Garlic 40
  65. Dilled Green Beans 41
  66. Dilly Beans 41
  67. Dilly Cheese Wheat Bread 42
  68. Dilly Round Steak 42
  69. Dilly Rye Boat Dip 43
  70. Dilly Tomato And Beet Salad 43
  71. Dilly-of-a-baked Potato Salad 43
  72. Easy Dill Hollandaise Sauce 44

3

73. Easy Lemony-dilly Cucumber Salad 45
74. Easy Potato Salad With Dill 45
75. Easy Roasted Potatoes 45
76. Fermented Kosher-style Dill Pickles 46
77. Feta & Herb Dip 47
78. Fish Baked En Croute De Sel (fish Baked In A Salt Crust) 47
79. Fresh Dill Pasta Salad 48
80. Fresh Herb & Lemon Bulgur Pilaf 48
81. Garbanzo Bean Salad Ii 49
82. Garden Fresh Salad 49
83. Garlic And Dill Salmon 50
84. Garlic Dill Burgers 50
85. Garlic Dill New Potatoes 50
86. George's Salmon-pepper Pate 51
87. Gluten Free And Paleo Tuna Avocado Cups 51
88. Golden Gazpacho Dip 52
89. Greek Yogurt-and-dill-marinated Chicken 52
90. Green Borscht 53
91. Grilled Salmon Sandwich With Dill Sauce 53
92. Grilled Salmon Sandwich With Green Apple Slaw 54
93. Hearty Cabbage-rutabaga Slow Cooker Soup 54
94. Herbed Feta Dip 55
95. Herbed Zucchini Soup 55
96. High Seas Chicken Souvlaki 56
97. Hot Off The Grill Potatoes 57
98. Hudson's Baked Tilapia With Dill Sauce 57
99. Hungarian Cucumber Salad 58
100. Jagic (assyrian Cheese Spread) 58
101. Jalapeño & Dill Labneh 58
102. Kohlrabi And Pea Soup With Dill 59
103. Kosher Chicken Soup With Matzo Balls 59
104. Kosher Seasoning Salt 60
105. Labneh (lebanese Yogurt) 61
106. Lamb And Potato Skillet 61
107. Lemon & Dill Chicken 62
108. Lemon Dill Salad Dressing 62
109. Lemon Dill Salmon Fillet 63
110. Mama H's Fooled You Fancy Slow Cooker Turkey Breast 63
111. Maple Dill Carrots 64
112. Mast-o-khiar 64
113. Meze Fava Beans 65
114. Mizeria (polish Cucumber Salad) 65
115. Mloda Kapusta Z Koperkiem (spring Cabbage With Dill) 66
116. Mom's Dill Dip 66
117. Mushroom Melt With Dill Aioli 66
118. Orzo Salad With Salmon, Herbs, And Yogurt Vinaigrette 67
119. Oven-baked Cod With Bread Crumbs . 67
120. Oven-baked Salmon With Herbs 68
121. Oven-roasted Fish With Peas And Tomatoes 68
122. Pan-seared Salmon With Fennel & Dill Salsa 69
123. Pasta With Creamy Smoked Salmon And Dill 70
124. Poached Halibut With Herbed Vinaigrette 70
125. Polish Zucchini Salad 71
126. Pop's Dill Pickles 71
127. Puff Pastry Chicken 'n Broccoli Pot Pie 72
128. Quick Poached Salmon With Dill Mustard Sauce 73
129. Quick Vegetarian Egg-lemon Soup With Brown Rice 73
130. Quinoa And Dill Flatbread 74
131. Ranch Dressing With Fresh Herbs 74
132. Refrigerator Dill Pickles 75
133. Refrigerator Garlic Dill Spears 75
134. Roasted Garlic & Herb Bread 76
135. Roasted Green Beans With Dill Vinaigrette 76
136. Salmon 'tartare' Spread 77
137. Salmon Bisque For Two 77
138. Salmon Cakes With Olives, Lemon & Dill 78
139. Salmon Dill Biscuits 78
140. Salmon En Papillote 79
141. Salmon Fillets With Creamy Dill 79
142. Salmon Patties With Dill Sauce 80
143. Salmon Salad 80
144. Salmon With Creamy Dill Sauce From Swanson® 81
145. Salmon With Lemon And Dill 81

146.	Salmon, Cream Cheese & Dill Souffle	82
147.	Savory Lemon Dill Parmesan Scones	83
148.	Shrimp And Dill Deviled Eggs	83
149.	Simple Herb Salad Mix	84
150.	Slow-roasted Whole Salmon	84
151.	Smoked Salmon & Dill Scones	85
152.	Smoked Salmon Dill Eggs Benedict	86
153.	Smoked Salmon Spread	86
154.	Smoked Trout Salad With Herb & Horseradish Dressing	87
155.	Sour Cream, Cucumber And Dill Dip	87
156.	Southern Dill Potato Salad	88
157.	Spicy Refrigerator Dill Pickles	88
158.	Spicy Shrimp And Red Bean Soup	89
159.	Spinach With Chickpeas And Fresh Dill	89
160.	Stuffed Bell Pepper Rings	89
161.	Summer Cucumber Salad	90
162.	Sweet And Sour Cabbage Soup	90
163.	Sweet Pea And Dill Salad	91
164.	Ta'ameya (egyptian Falafel)	92
165.	Tailgate Potato Salad	92
166.	The Brutus Salad	93
167.	Three-herb Potato Salad	93
168.	Tuna Pasta Salad With Dill	94
169.	Tuna Salad With Fresh Dill	94
170.	Vegan Dill Pasta Salad	95
171.	Vegan Pasta Salad	95
172.	Vegan Ranch Dressing	96
173.	Walnut, Dill & Tuna Salad	96
174.	Wheat Berry Salad With Peas, Radishes, And Dill	97
175.	Zucchini And Tomato Casserole	97

INDEX 99

CONCLUSION 106

Introduction

***

Why I Love Cooking

Hi all,

Welcome to MrandMsCooking.com—a website created by a community of cooking enthusiasts with the goal of providing books for novice cooks featuring the best recipes, at the most affordable prices, and valuable gifts.

Before we go to the recipes in the book "Hello! 175 Dill Recipes", I have an interesting story to share with you the reason for loving cooking.

My mom would always tell me:

Cooking is an edible form of love…

As a young kid, I helped my mom cook. She would always cook any dish I liked. Observing how she cooked motivated me to try cooking. Ten years later, I'm sharing with you my cooking inspiration as well as the reasons why I love it.

1. Trying something different

Various cuisines of the world use different kinds of ingredients. You can download and share a lot of recipes on the internet. Even so, you can add your own unique twists to recipes and experiment with various versions and styles.

Trying out new recipes and ingredients isn't bad when cooking, as long as you produce something edible…

2. Enjoyment

Whomever you cook for— family, friends, or even yourself—you'll surely have fun doing it. It's satisfying to see how the combination of various spices, meat, and vegetables yield an awesome flavor. From cutting to cooking them, the whole process is nothing but pure joy.

3. Receiving wonderful feedback

Don't you get a sense of pride, joy, and accomplishment when people love the dish you've cooked and let you know their thoughts? You'll definitely savor the moment when you hear someone praise your cooking skills.

Each time someone tells me, "This has a great flavor" or "This is insanely delicious!" I get more motivated to become a better cook…

4. Healthy eating

Rather than consuming processed food, using fresh ingredients for your dishes makes them good for the body. Cook your own meals so that you can add more fresh vegetables and fruits to your diet. Cooking also allows you to discover more about the different nutrients in your meals.

Because you prepare your meals yourself, having digestive problems will be the least of your worries…

5. Therapeutic activity

Based on my experience, cooking calms the mind. Finding food in the fridge, gathering the ingredients, getting them ready, and assembling everything together to create a yummy dish are more relaxing than just spending idle time on the couch watching TV. Cooking never makes me stressed.

My mother would always tell me: Cooking is an edible way to make your loved ones feel loved…

Keeping Up Your Passion for Cooking

Cooking is not for everyone. But people who are passionate about cooking and their families are fortunate indeed. It spreads happiness around. Do you love cooking? Sustain your passion—it's the best feeling ever!

When combined with love, cooking feeds the soul…

From my unending love for cooking, I'm creating this book series and hoping to share my passion with all of you. With my many experiences of failures, I have created this book series and hopefully it helps you. This Ingredient Recipes Series covers these subjects:

- Cheese Recipes
- Butter Recipes
- Red Wine Recipes
- Cajun Spice Recipes
- Mayonnaise Recipes
- ...

I really appreciate that you have selected "Hello! 175 Dill Recipes" and for reading to the end. I anticipate that this book shall give you the source of strength during the times that you are really exhausted, as well as be your best friend in the comforts of your own home. Please also give me some love by sharing your own exciting cooking time in the comments segment below.

List of Abbreviations

LIST OF ABBREVIATIONS	
tbsp(s).	tablespoon(s)
tsp(s).	teaspoon(s)
c.	cup(s)
oz.	ounce(s)
lb(s).	pound(s)

175 Amazing Dill Recipes

***

1. 'i Hate Cucumbers!' Cucumber Salad

"If you want crunch, you can cut the vegetables thicker."
Serving: 10 | Prep: 25m | Ready in: 1h25m

Ingredients

- 1/2 cup red wine vinegar
- 2 teaspoons white sugar
- 1/2 teaspoon black pepper
- 1 teaspoon dried dill weed
- 1/4 cup mayonnaise
- 5 cucumbers, scored and thinly sliced
- 1 stalk celery, thinly sliced
- 1/2 red onion, chopped
- salt to taste

Direction

- In a big bowl, combine dill, pepper, sugar, and vinegar until the sugar is melted. Mix in mayonnaise until creamy, and then add red onion, celery, and cucumbers until evenly blended with the dressing. Put a cover on and chill for a minimum of 1 hour. Use salt to season and toss some more before eating.

Nutrition Information

- Calories: 71 calories;
- Total Carbohydrate: 7.7 g
- Cholesterol: 2 mg
- Total Fat: 4.5 g
- Protein: 1.1 g
- Sodium: 38 mg

2. 20-minute Skillet Salmon

"Sizzling salmon served with creamy sauce."
Serving: 4 | Prep: 10m | Ready in: 20m

Ingredients

- 4 (4 ounce) salmon fillets
- 1 cup fat-free milk
- 1/2 cup PHILADELPHIA 1/3 Less Fat than Cream Cheese
- 2 cups chopped cucumbers
- 2 tablespoons chopped fresh dill
- 2 cups hot cooked long-grain white rice

Direction

- Use cooking spray for spraying a large skillet then heat it on medium-high heat. Add in fish and allow each side to cook for 5 minutes until fish easily flakes with a fork. Remove from skillet; keep warm by covering.
- In skillet, add reduced-fat cream cheese and milk; cook and stir till cream cheese is melted completely and mixture is blended well. Add in dill and cucumbers and stir.
- Return fish back to skillet. Cook until thoroughly heated for 2 minutes. Serve with rice and cream cheese sauce on top.

Nutrition Information

- Calories: 295 calories;
- Total Carbohydrate: 27.8 g
- Cholesterol: 64 mg
- Total Fat: 7.6 g
- Protein: 27.2 g
- Sodium: 79 mg

3. A Lot More Than Plain Spinach Pie (Greek Batsaria)

"This recipe is a collection of greens and combined with feta cheese. It takes a long time to make and contains no leftovers but believe me, you will not be disappointed.""
Serving: 9 | Prep: 50m | Ready in: 1h50m

Ingredients

- 3 eggs
- 1 pound chopped fresh spinach
- 3 leeks, chopped
- 5 green onions, chopped
- 2 1/3 cups crumbled feta cheese
- 1 bunch parsley, chopped
- 1 bunch dill, chopped
- 1 bunch spearmint, chopped
- 1 teaspoon white sugar
- 1 cup milk
- 3/4 cup olive oil
- 1 pinch salt and ground black pepper to taste
- 2 1/2 cups all-purpose flour
- 1/2 cup semolina flour
- 1 pinch salt
- 1/4 cup olive oil
- 2 cups water
- 1 1/4 cups grated Parmesan cheese (optional)
- 2 tablespoons cold butter, cut into pieces
- 2 tablespoons olive oil

Direction

- Turn oven to 350°F (175°C to preheat). Lightly oil a deep 9x9-inch baking dish.
- In a mixing bowl, beat eggs, then mix in 3/4 cup olive oil, milk, sugar, spearmint, dill, parsley, feta cheese, green onions, leeks, and spinach until well combined. Add pepper and salt to taste; put to one side. In another mixing bowl, combine 1 pinch of salt, semolina flour, and all-purpose flour. Mix in water and 1/4 cup olive oil until smooth. Transfer two-thirds of the batter into the greased 9x9-inch baking dish, distribute evenly. Ladle spinach filling over the cake batter, then pour the rest of the batter over the top of the whole thing. Add 2 tablespoons of olive oil, butter pieces, and Parmesan cheese on top.
- Bake for about 1 hour in the preheated oven until the bottom crust and the surface has set and beautifully browned.

Nutrition Information

- Calories: 650 calories;
- Total Carbohydrate: 45 g
- Cholesterol: 115 mg
- Total Fat: 44.1 g
- Protein: 20.1 g
- Sodium: 714 mg

4. Afghan Tomato Soup (Aush Goshti)

"This recipe is my attempt to re-create a soup I've once tried at a restaurant. This soup is loaded with dill flavors and very lemony."
Serving: 8 | Prep: 15m | Ready in: 1h30m

Ingredients

- 1 tablespoon butter
- 1 onion, chopped
- 3 cloves garlic, minced
- 1/2 pound ground beef
- 1 (6 ounce) can tomato paste
- 1 (32 ounce) can tomato juice
- 5 cups water
- 1 (15 ounce) can garbanzo beans, drained and coarsely chopped
- 1 (16 ounce) package uncooked fettuccine
- 1/2 teaspoon salt
- 1/2 teaspoon ground black pepper
- 1 teaspoon dry mustard
- 1 tablespoon chopped fresh dill
- 1 tablespoon chopped fresh cilantro, or to taste
- 1 teaspoon chili paste, or to taste
- 2 teaspoons fresh lemon juice, or to taste

Direction

- In a big pot, heat butter over medium heat. Cook onions in butter for 10 minutes until the onions start to get tender. Mix in garlic and cook for 1 minute. Add ground beef and cook for 10-15 minutes until the beef is not pink anymore; tossing sometimes to crumble into chunks. Mix in garbanzo beans, water, tomato juice, and tomato paste. Use lemon juice, chili paste, cilantro, dill, dry mustard, pepper, and salt to season. Boil, and then lower the heat to low. Simmer without a cover for 30 minutes.
- Raise the heat and boil the mixture to low boil, add fettuccine, lower the heat to medium-low and cook for 10 minutes until the fettuccine is soft. Adjust the seasonings, adding extra lemon juice, salt, or chile paste if you want. Add a little water to thin out if the soup seems too thick.

Nutrition Information

- Calories: 383 calories;
- Total Carbohydrate: 62.9 g
- Cholesterol: 21 mg
- Total Fat: 7.4 g
- Protein: 17.1 g
- Sodium: 764 mg

5. Angie's Dilly Casserole Bread

"This delicious bread is a family recipe. Toast it with lots of butter for better flavor.""
Serving: 8 | Prep: 15m | Ready in: 2h20m

Ingredients

- 1 (.25 ounce) package active dry yeast
- 1/4 cup warm water
- 1 cup cottage cheese, room temperature
- 2 tablespoons white sugar
- 1 tablespoon butter, room temperature, plus more as needed
- 1 teaspoon salt
- 1/4 teaspoon baking soda
- 2 teaspoons dill seed
- 1 tablespoon dried minced onion
- 1 egg
- 2 1/4 cups all-purpose flour, or more if needed
- 1 pinch salt

Direction

- Steep yeast in warm water to soften, about 10 minutes.
- In a large mixing bowl, combine baking soda, 1 teaspoon salt, butter, sugar, and cottage cheese. Add yeast mixture, egg, dried onion, and dill seed, and stir well. Slowly add 1/4 cup flour at a time until finished, mixing well after each addition. Add additional 1 or 2 tablespoons of flour if dough is too sticky.
- Us a clean cotton kitchen towel to cover the bowl and place the bowl in a warm place for about 1 hour or until double in size.
- Set oven to 350°F (175°C) to preheat. Grease a 1-1/2 to 2-quart baking dish with a generous amount of butter.
- Stir the dough gently to release bubbles. Remove the dough to the greased baking dish. Bring to bake for about 35 minutes in the preheated oven until the bread turns golden brown. Take out of the oven, brush butter over the top of the bread and sprinkle with a pinch of salt. Allow bread to cool for 5 minutes then transfer it to a cooling rack to cool.

Nutrition Information

- Calories: 196 calories;
- Total Carbohydrate: 31.7 g
- Cholesterol: 31 mg
- Total Fat: 3.8 g
- Protein: 8.4 g
- Sodium: 484 mg

6. Arakas Latheros (Greek Peas With Tomato And Dill)

"Peas can be served as a main dish in Greece. Enjoy this dish with crusty bread and feta cheese for a hearty meal.""
Serving: 4 | Prep: 10m | Ready in: 50m

Ingredients

- 3 tablespoons olive oil
- 6 green onions, chopped
- 1 (16 ounce) package frozen peas
- 1 cup crushed tomatoes
- 1 potato, peeled and cut into wedges
- 1/2 cup chopped fresh dill
- 1/2 cup water (optional)
- salt and ground black pepper to taste

Direction

- In a saucepan, heat olive oil over medium heat and sauté onion for about 5 minutes until soft yet not browned. Add potato, tomatoes, peas, and dill; sprinkle with pepper and salt for seasoning. If there is not enough liquid from the tomatoes, add more water.
- Mix well and bring to a boil. Reduce heat and cook, partly covered for about 30 minutes until potato and peas are tender. Make sure that all the liquid from the tomatoes has vaporized before serving.

Nutrition Information

- Calories: 245 calories;
- Total Carbohydrate: 31 g
- Cholesterol: 0 mg
- Total Fat: 10.8 g
- Protein: 8.5 g
- Sodium: 255 mg

7. Artichokes With Lemon & Dill

"You can enjoy these artichokes cold or at room temperature. This dish can be a great side dish with grilled fish or chicken and it can be the first course."
Serving: 8 | Ready in: 50m

Ingredients

- 4 large lemons, divided, plus more for garnish
- 8 large artichokes
- 2 cups water
- 6 cloves garlic, chopped
- ¼ cup chopped fresh dill, plus more for garnish
- 1 teaspoon salt
- ¼ teaspoon ground pepper
- 1½ tablespoons extra-virgin olive oil

Direction

- Extract juice from 2 lemons. In a big bowl, fill cold water and add juice and the rinds. Trim the bottom 1/4 inch off the artichoke stems with a paring knife. Use kitchen scissors to snip the thorn off the leaves. Chop approximately 1 inch from the tops. Use a spoon or a melon baller to remove the fuzzy chokes. To avoid discoloration, put the trimmed artichokes in the lemon water.
- Extract 1/3 cup of juice from the last 2 lemons. In a big nonreactive pot large enough to contain the artichokes in one layer, mix 2 cups of water with the lemon juice. Strain the artichokes and put them with their sides turning down in the pot. Put pepper, salt, dill, and garlic on top. Boil it. Lower the heat to low, put a cover on and simmer for 18-20 minutes, flip the artichokes 1 time, until soft enough for a fork to pierce them.
- Move the artichokes to a deep plate using a slotted spoon. Simmer the rest of the liquid in the pan over medium-high heat for 10 minutes until the liquid decrease to 1 1/4 cups. Ladle over the artichokes. Allow cooling to room temperature.

- Use oil to drizzle and sauce to baste the artichokes to enjoy. Use lemon wedges and chopped dill to garnish if you want.

Nutrition Information

- Calories: 105 calories;
- Total Carbohydrate: 18 g
- Cholesterol: 0 mg
- Total Fat: 3 g
- Fiber: 9 g
- Protein: 5 g
- Sodium: 444 mg
- Sugar: 2 g
- Saturated Fat: 0 g

8. Australian Potato Salad

"This is a simple but perfect potato salad with the addition of a hint of mint to blow away the heat on a hot summer day."
Serving: 16 | Prep: 20m | Ready in: 50m

Ingredients

- 4 pounds white potatoes, cut into 1 inch cubes
- 3/4 cup bottled French salad dressing
- 1 cup chopped celery
- 6 green onions, chopped
- 1 1/4 cups mayonnaise
- 1 cup sour cream
- 1 tablespoon coarse grained mustard
- 1/2 cup chopped fresh mint leaves
- 1/2 cup chopped fresh dill weed
- ground black pepper to taste

Direction

- In a big pot, put potatoes and sufficient water to cover. Bring to a boil without a cover, then take away from heat, cover and allow to stand for 25 minutes. Drain and move to a serving bowl. While the potatoes are still warm, stir in French salad dressing, then let it cool for a minimum of 1 hour.
- Put the green onions and celery into the potatoes, then stir in pepper, dill, mint, mustard, sour cream and mayonnaise. Chill until serving.

Nutrition Information

- Calories: 291 calories;
- Total Carbohydrate: 21.8 g
- Cholesterol: 13 mg
- Total Fat: 22.1 g
- Protein: 2.8 g
- Sodium: 229 mg

9. Baba's Best Sorrel Soup

"This hearty soup is loaded with flavors. My father-in-law said that it tasted like his mom's soup. Fresh sorrel in the spring will make this soup taste its best. You can enjoy this soup with biscuits or crusty bread and top it with cilantro, dill, parsley, or any kinds of herbs that you like."
Serving: 4 | Prep: 25m | Ready in: 1h35m

Ingredients

- 1/2 cup unsalted butter
- 1 cup sliced onion
- 5 large cloves garlic, minced
- 12 cups tightly packed sorrel leaves, stems and veins removed
- 4 cups chicken stock
- 2 cups water
- 3 potatoes, peeled and diced
- 1 large carrot, peeled and cut into matchsticks
- 1 cup chopped fresh parsley
- 3 sprigs fresh dill, chopped, or to taste
- 1 tablespoon lemon juice
- 1 teaspoon freshly ground black pepper
- 1/4 teaspoon ground cayenne pepper, or more to taste

Direction

- In a big Dutch oven, heat butter over medium heat. Add garlic and onion, stir and cook for 5 minutes until tender. Add sorrel in batches,

- tossing thoroughly for 5-8 minutes in total until wilted.
- Add water and chicken stock to the Dutch oven. Mix in cayenne pepper, black pepper, lemon juice, dill, parsley, carrot, and potatoes. Simmer the soup for 1 hour until the flavors blend.
- Use an immersion blender to puree the soup until nearly smooth then enjoy.

Nutrition Information

- Calories: 379 calories;
- Total Carbohydrate: 37.5 g
- Cholesterol: 66 mg
- Total Fat: 23.9 g
- Protein: 5.9 g
- Sodium: 1000 mg

10. Baby Carrots With Dill Butter

"You can enjoy this dish with any meats."
Serving: 8 | Prep: 10m | Ready in: 20m

Ingredients

- 1 (16 ounce) package baby carrots
- 2 tablespoons margarine
- 1 tablespoon chopped fresh dill
- 1 tablespoon fresh lemon juice
- 1/4 teaspoon salt
- 1/8 teaspoon freshly ground black pepper

Direction

- In a saucepan, put carrots and cover with enough water. Boil it and cook until soft, about 10 minutes. Take away from heat, and strain. Lightly mix with lemon juice, dill, and margarine. Use pepper and salt to season.

Nutrition Information

- Calories: 44 calories;
- Total Carbohydrate: 4.9 g
- Cholesterol: 0 mg
- Total Fat: 2.7 g
- Protein: 0.4 g
- Sodium: 148 mg

11. Baked Halibut Sitka

"A fantastic moist halibut recipe."
Serving: 6 | Prep: 10m | Ready in: 35m

Ingredients

- 2 pounds halibut fillet, cut into 6 pieces
- salt and ground black pepper to taste
- 1 bunch green onions, chopped
- 1/2 cup mayonnaise
- 1/2 cup sour cream
- 1 teaspoon dried dill weed

Direction

- Preheat an oven to 245°C/475°F.
- Grease the 9x13-in. baking dish.
- Use ground black pepper and salt to season halibut.
- In greased baking dish, put halibut.
- In a bowl, mix dill, sour cream, mayonnaise and green onions.
- Evenly spread green onion mixture on every halibut piece.
- In preheated oven, bake for 20 minutes till it easily flakes with a fork and fish is opaque.
- Take out of oven. Before serving, let stand for 5 minutes.

Nutrition Information

- Calories: 354 calories;
- Total Carbohydrate: 4.2 g
- Cholesterol: 72 mg
- Total Fat: 21.5 g
- Protein: 33.8 g
- Sodium: 205 mg

12. Barney's King Salmon Gravlax

"I created this king salmon gravlax after many trials over the years. Simple is good. The results are reliable and repeatable. Great together with honey-mustard-dill sauce."
Serving: 10 | Prep: 15m | Ready in: 1day12h15m

Ingredients

- 1 cup dark brown sugar
- 3/4 cup kosher salt
- 2 tablespoons cracked white peppercorns
- 2 (1 pound) salmon fillets, bones removed
- 1 bunch fresh dill, finely chopped

Direction

- In a bowl, mix peppercorns, salt, and sugar and combine well. Drizzle about 1/3 of mixture on the bottom of a glass baking dish. Put one salmon fillet on top with the skin-side down. Top with a drizzle of 1/2 the dill. Add another 1/3 of sugar mixture to cover. Drizzle the remaining dill onto the second fillet and put skin-side up onto the first fillet. Pour the remaining sugar mixture to cover.
- Use plastic wrap to wrap the baking dish tightly and then chill for 18 hours. Flip the fillets over and ladle the syrupy liquid on top of fish before you cover once again using plastic wrap. Chill for another 18 hours.
- Lightly rinse the fillets with cold water to get rid of salt and then pat dry. Thinly chop the fish at an angle.

Nutrition Information

- Calories: 255 calories;
- Total Carbohydrate: 22.8 g
- Cholesterol: 54 mg
- Total Fat: 9.9 g
- Protein: 18.3 g
- Sodium: 6893 mg

13. Beef Pirozhki

"When I was a bike messenger, I would go for a beef pirozhki from one of the delis in the city and they cost me 2 bucks. I loved the beef and had lots of calories. I decided to copy-cat the recipe to keep the experience."
Serving: 15 | Prep: 1h | Ready in: 2h35m

Ingredients

- For the Dough:
- 1 cup warm milk (110 degrees F)
- 1 (.25 ounce) package active dry yeast
- 2 teaspoons white sugar
- 1 teaspoon kosher salt
- 1 large egg, beaten
- 2 tablespoons melted butter
- 3 cups all-purpose flour, or as needed
- 1/2 teaspoon oil, or as needed
- For the Beef Filling:
- 1 tablespoon olive oil
- 1 tablespoon butter
- 1 large onion, finely diced
- 2 pounds ground beef
- 2 teaspoons kosher salt, or more to taste
- 1/2 teaspoon freshly ground black pepper
- 4 cloves garlic, minced
- 2 teaspoons dried dill weed
- 1/3 cup chicken broth
- 1/4 cup shredded sharp Cheddar cheese (optional)
- 2 tablespoons grated Parmesan cheese (optional)
- vegetable oil for frying

Direction

- Mix yeast and one scant cup of warm milk in the bowl of stand mixer that is fitted with a dough hook. Leave to stand for about 10 minutes until bubbly and foamy. Add almost all of the flour, butter, egg, salt and sugar. Reserving a little amount in case the dough gets too dry.
- Then knead in the mixer until the dough is supple and soft. Scrape the dough over the work surface. Use a few drops of oil to coat the bowl and then return the dough. Cover the

- bowl and allow the dough to rise in a warm area for about 1 hour until doubled in volume.
- Meanwhile, over medium-high heat, heat butter and olive oil in a pot. Add garlic, ground beef, and onion. Season with black pepper and kosher salt. Cook the beef while breaking apart using a wooden spoon for 5 to 7 minutes until no pink color remains. Continue to cook while stirring sometime for about 2 minutes until browned evenly. Take out from the heat source.
- Mix the dill into beef mixture. Stir in chicken broth and scrape up browned bits from the pan's bottom. Allow the mixture to cool for ten minutes. Mix in Parmesan cheese and Cheddar cheese. Leave the filling to cool completely.
- Place the dough onto a work surface and squeeze out air bubbles. Pinch a piece of dough off and shape into a ball and then press into a disc. Sprinkle with a minimal amount flour and then roll to form a circle of 5 to 6 inches in diameter and about 1/8-inch thick. Immerse your finger in water and then moisten the edges of the circle.
- Place the dough circle in one hand and then pour in several tablespoons of beef filling. Seal by pinching the edges together. Put the pirozhki on the table with the seam-side up and then pinch off the excess dough. It is hard to fry with too much dough. Use water to moisten the middle of the seam. Then fold the two ends inward and turn the pirozhki over with the seam-side down. Push down lightly.
- Gather the remaining pirozhki and leave them to stand for 15 to 20 minutes until the dough rises a bit.
- Heat the oil in a large saucepan or deep-fryer to 190 degrees C (375 degrees F). Fry the pirozhki in batches, with the seam-side down, for about 90 seconds until turned golden brown. Turn and then fry for about 90 seconds until browned on the other side. Place on paper towels to drain and then cool for a few minutes.

Nutrition Information

- Calories: 293 calories;
- Total Carbohydrate: 22 g
- Cholesterol: 59 mg
- Total Fat: 16.1 g
- Protein: 14.3 g
- Sodium: 486 mg

14. Best Buckwheat Salad

"This dish is tasty and healthy."
Serving: 6 | Prep: 20m | Ready in: 35m

Ingredients

- 2 cups water
- 1 cup buckwheat
- 1 lime, juiced
- 1 red onion, chopped
- 1 tomato, chopped
- 1/2 cup chopped pitted Kalamata olives
- 1 bunch fresh mint, chopped
- 1/2 bunch fresh dill, chopped
- 2 tablespoons olive oil
- 1 tablespoon rice-wine vinegar
- 1 teaspoon ground cumin
- salt and ground black pepper to taste
- 1/3 cup feta cheese

Direction

- In a saucepan, mix together buckwheat and water, boil it. Lower the heat; simmer for 10 minutes until the buckwheat has absorbed the water.
- In a bowl, pour lime juice. Add dill, mint, Kalamata olives, tomato, and onion. Mix in pepper, salt, cumin, rice-wine vinegar, and olive oil. Add buckwheat, tossing until ingredients blend. Put feta cheese on top.

Nutrition Information

- Calories: 224 calories;
- Total Carbohydrate: 25.6 g
- Cholesterol: 12 mg
- Total Fat: 11.7 g
- Protein: 6.8 g

- Sodium: 373 mg

15. Best-ever Cucumber Dill Salad

"Creating this recipe was just an accident."
Serving: 6 | Prep: 15m | Ready in: 25m

Ingredients

- 1/2 cucumber, very thinly sliced
- salt and ground black pepper to taste
- 1/4 cup sour cream, or to taste
- 1/4 cup vinegar, or more to taste
- 1/4 cup plain yogurt
- 2 tablespoons mayonnaise
- 1/2 lime, juiced
- 2 teaspoons white sugar
- 1 teaspoon dill
- 1/2 red onion, thinly sliced
- 1/2 stalk celery, thinly sliced

Direction

- In a strainer, put cucumber slices. Use salt to drizzle liberally over the cucumber; let stand for 10 minutes until the water begins to draw out from the slices. Strain the water from the cucumber slices.
- In a big bowl, combine dill, sugar, lime juice, mayonnaise, yogurt, vinegar, and sour cream until the dressing is creamy. Toss celery, onion, and cucumber into the dressing until evenly combined, use pepper and salt to season.

Nutrition Information

- Calories: 75 calories;
- Total Carbohydrate: 5.1 g
- Cholesterol: 7 mg
- Total Fat: 5.9 g
- Protein: 1.2 g
- Sodium: 42 mg

16. Big Ray's Paleo Roasted Cauliflower

"Your kids will love to eat their vegetables with this dish."
Serving: 6 | Prep: 10m | Ready in: 35m

Ingredients

- cooking spray
- 2 tablespoons olive oil
- 1 1/2 teaspoons dried dill weed
- 2 cloves garlic, minced
- 1 teaspoon lemon juice
- 1/2 teaspoon ground cumin
- 1/4 teaspoon salt
- 1/4 teaspoon ground black pepper
- 1 large head cauliflower, cut into florets

Direction

- Start preheating the oven to 450°F (230°C). Use cooking spray to grease a 2-quart glass casserole pan.
- In a bowl, combine pepper, salt, cumin, lemon juice, garlic, dill, and olive oil. Add cauliflower, toss until blended. Spread in the prepared pan.
- Put in the preheated oven and roast for 25 minutes, flipping halfway through, until soft. Move to a dish; ladle any remaining juices in the plate on top.

Nutrition Information

- Calories: 78 calories;
- Total Carbohydrate: 8.1 g
- Cholesterol: 0 mg
- Total Fat: 4.7 g
- Protein: 2.9 g
- Sodium: 140 mg

17. Brown Butter & Dill Brussels Sprouts

"Adding a bit of Brussels sprouts will make this dish taste even more delicious."
Serving: 4 | Ready in: 25m

Ingredients

- 1 pound Brussels sprouts, trimmed and quartered
- 1 tablespoon unsalted butter
- 1 tablespoon extra-virgin olive oil
- 3 tablespoons slivered almonds, toasted (see Tip)
- 1 tablespoon white-wine vinegar
- 1 tablespoon chopped fresh dill or 1 teaspoon dried
- ¼ teaspoon salt
- ¼ teaspoon freshly ground pepper

Direction

- Fit a steamer basket in a big saucepan, add 1 inch of water and boil. Add Brussels sprouts, put a cover on and steam for 5-7 minutes until soft.
- In the meantime, in a small frying pan, heat butter over medium heat. Cook, swirling frequently for 1-3 minutes until the butter has a nutty browned color. Mix in oil and use a rubber spatula to scrape into a big bowl. Add pepper, salt, dill, vinegar, almonds, and Brussels sprouts.

Nutrition Information

- Calories: 131 calories;
- Total Carbohydrate: 10 g
- Cholesterol: 8 mg
- Total Fat: 10 g
- Fiber: 4 g
- Protein: 4 g
- Sodium: 172 mg
- Sugar: 2 g
- Saturated Fat: 3 g

18. Cabbage Veggie Cream Soup

"This soup is super tasty. The ingredients may sound too bizarre with Tabasco® and vinegar, but the result will surprise you. Put some sour cream on top to enjoy."
Serving: 8 | Prep: 40m | Ready in: 1h40m

Ingredients

- 1 pound elk breakfast sausage
- 2 tablespoons olive oil
- 3 cloves garlic, minced
- 2 teaspoons minced fresh ginger root
- 1 onion, chopped
- 2 cups cubed butternut squash
- 2 beets, sliced into rounds
- 4 red potatoes, diced
- 4 carrots, chopped
- 1/2 medium head green cabbage, chopped
- 1 teaspoon hot pepper sauce (such as Tabasco®), or to taste
- 2 teaspoons dried dill weed
- 2 teaspoons dried rubbed sage
- 2 teaspoons dried thyme leaves
- salt and black pepper to taste
- 2 quarts chicken broth
- 1 (10.75 ounce) can condensed cream of mushroom soup
- 1/4 cup red wine vinegar

Direction

- Heat a big pot over medium-high heat. Stir and cook sausage in the heated pot until not pink anymore, turns evenly browned, and crumbly. Strain and dispose any extra fat, saving the browned sausage.
- Add olive oil to the pot, mix in cabbage, carrots, red potatoes, beets, butternut squash, onion, ginger, and garlic. Stir and cook for 10 minutes. Use pepper, salt, thyme, sage, dill, and hot pepper sauce to season. Add vinegar, cream of mushroom soup, chicken broth, and the browned sausage. Simmer over high heat. Lower the heat to medium-low, put a cover on, and simmer for 30 minutes until all vegetables are soft.

Nutrition Information

- Calories: 196 calories;
- Total Carbohydrate: 22 g
- Cholesterol: 26 mg
- Total Fat: 6.6 g
- Protein: 13.8 g
- Sodium: 323 mg

19. Carrot Dill Soup

"This soup is made of fresh dill and pureed carrots. You can use 1/3 of the amount for dried herbs instead of fresh herbs."

Serving: 6 | Prep: 10m | Ready in: 45m

Ingredients

- 1 pound carrots, sliced
- 2 teaspoons vegetable oil
- 2 teaspoons minced garlic
- 1 cup chopped onion
- 3 1/2 cups chicken stock
- 3/4 cup 2% milk
- 2 tablespoons chopped fresh dill
- 2 tablespoons chopped fresh chives

Direction

- Boil a big saucepan of water. Add carrots, and cook until just soft. Strain, and put the carrots back to the pan. Put aside.
- In a frying pan, heat oil over medium heat. Sauté garlic and onion for 5 minutes until tender. Put the garlic and onion into the carrots in the saucepan, and add chicken stock. Turn the heat to medium-low, put a cover on, and simmer until the flavors blend, about 25 minutes.
- In a blender or a food processor, put the carrot mixture and puree, working in small batches if needed. Put back to the saucepan, and mix in chives, dill, and milk. Cook until just thoroughly heated, and enjoy.

Nutrition Information

- Calories: 70 calories;
- Total Carbohydrate: 10.9 g
- Cholesterol: 2 mg
- Total Fat: 2.3 g
- Protein: 2.1 g
- Sodium: 66 mg

20. Chanterelle Mushroom And Wild Rice Soup

"You can switch this recipe up with different rice combos and mushrooms."

Serving: 4 | Prep: 15m | Ready in: 58m

Ingredients

- 1 tablespoon olive oil
- 1 onion, chopped
- 1/2 head garlic, minced
- 5 cups fresh chanterelle mushrooms, or more to taste
- 1 cup wild rice
- 4 cups chicken broth, or more to taste
- 3 tablespoons soy sauce
- 2 tablespoons lemon juice
- 1 tablespoon dried parsley
- 2 teaspoons ground black pepper
- 2 teaspoons dill
- 1 teaspoon ground paprika
- 1 teaspoon salt, or more to taste

Direction

- In big pot, heat olive oil on medium low heat. Add garlic and onion; mix and cook for 2 minutes till soft yet not browned. Add chanterelle mushrooms; mix and cook for 5-10 minutes till excess liquid evaporates. Mix wild rice in; mix and cook for 1-2 minutes.
- Put broth in pot; boil soup. Lower heat to low; simmer for 20-30 minutes till mushrooms are tender. Mix salt, paprika, dill, black pepper, parsley, lemon juice and soy sauce in; simmer for 10 minutes till flavors combine.

Nutrition Information

- Calories: 306 calories;
- Total Carbohydrate: 51.6 g
- Cholesterol: 5 mg
- Total Fat: 4.5 g
- Protein: 13.1 g
- Sodium: 2268 mg

21. Chateaubriand Con Vino Brodo

"Use the extra sauce for roasted veggies and potatoes."
Serving: 4 | Prep: 15m | Ready in: 1h5m

Ingredients

- 1 pound beef tenderloin roast, trimmed
- 2 cloves garlic, quartered
- 1/4 cup extra virgin olive oil
- 1 tablespoon lemon or lime juice
- 1 pinch dried oregano
- 1 pinch dried basil
- 1 pinch dried dill
- 1 pinch dried rosemary
- 1 pinch dried thyme
- 2 tablespoons whole multi-colored peppercorns
- 1 cup water
- 2 tablespoons Dijon mustard
- 1 clove chopped fresh garlic
- 1/4 cup butter
- 1 1/2 cups dry red wine

Direction

- Preheat an oven to 190°C/375°F.
- In roast, cut 8 small slits. Put garlic in slits.
- Mix thyme, rosemary, dill, basil, oregano, lemon juice and olive oil in medium bowl. Brush on roast. Press whole peppercorns into roast with a small spoon. Put roast on a rack in a roasting pan; put water into the bottom of the pan.
- In preheated oven, bake 40 minutes for well done or 20 minutes for medium rare. Transfer roast to cutting board; let sit for 5 minutes.
- Put drippings from roast into small saucepan on low heat. Mix butter, chopped garlic and mustard in; cook till butter melts completely. Add wine; reduce by half. Put sauce on sliced roast.

Nutrition Information

- Calories: 647 calories;
- Total Carbohydrate: 7.7 g
- Cholesterol: 111 mg
- Total Fat: 51.8 g
- Protein: 21 g
- Sodium: 330 mg

22. Cheese Torte With Chicken And Mushroom

"Russians love this multi-layered savory crepe cake. It is made up of 2 kinds of cheesy crepes and is filled with cream cheese, cheese, and mushrooms."
Serving: 10 | Prep: 30m | Ready in: 1h30m

Ingredients

- For the Crepes:
- 4 eggs
- 3/4 cup mayonnaise
- 2 tablespoons mayonnaise
- 3 cups shredded Gouda cheese
- 5 tablespoons all-purpose flour
- 1 bunch fresh dill, finely chopped
- 1 tablespoon vegetable oil
- 1 carrot, grated
- For the Filling:
- 1 tablespoon vegetable oil, or as needed
- 1 onion, diced
- 1 (10 ounce) package fresh mushrooms, chopped
- salt and ground black pepper to taste
- 1 (8 ounce) package cream cheese, softened
- 1/2 cup mayonnaise
- 2 cloves garlic, finely chopped
- 2 sprigs fresh dill, chopped, or to taste
- 1 (10 ounce) package diced cooked chicken

- 1 cucumber, thinly sliced

Direction

- In a bowl, whisk eggs with a 3/4 cup and 2 tbsp. of mayonnaise. Stir in flour and Gouda cheese. Transfer 1/2 of the batter in a separate bowl.
- Place the skillet over medium heat and heat 1 tbsp. of oil. Cook and stir grated carrot for 5 minutes until softened. Add the carrot into 1 portion of the batter. In another portion, add a small bunch of dill and mix.
- Place the nonstick or well-seasoned cast iron skillet over medium-low heat. Drop 2 tbsp. of one portion of the batter. Rotate the pan in circular motion immediately to spread evenly. Let it cook for 1-2 minutes until all edges are crispy. Flip it over and cook the other side for 1-2 more minutes until dry and browned. Do the same with the remaining batters, ending with a stack of carrot crepes and a stack of dill crepes.
- Place another skillet over medium-low heat and heat 1 tbsp. of oil. Cook the onion for 5 minutes, stirring constantly until soft and translucent. Add the mushrooms and cook for 5 more minutes until the liquid evaporates. Remove the mixture from heat and season with pepper and salt.
- In a bowl, whisk a 1/2 cup of mayonnaise and cream cheese. Season it with pepper and salt. Stir in 2 sprigs of dill and garlic.
- Spread the cream cheese mixture over the dill crepe. Layer it with mushroom-onion mixture. Top the layer with a carrot crepe. Spread more cream cheese and top it with chicken. Use all the crepes by repeating the layers. Garnish it with cucumber that is sliced thinly. Cover the crepes with plastic wrap and chill. Serve.

Nutrition Information

- Calories: 561 calories;
- Total Carbohydrate: 9.2 g
- Cholesterol: 173 mg
- Total Fat: 48.8 g
- Protein: 23 g

- Sodium: 603 mg

23. Chef Bevski's Greek Salad

"This dish was a hit for gatherings"
Serving: 8 | Prep: 30m | Ready in: 1h30m

Ingredients

- 3/4 cup olive oil
- 1/4 cup red wine vinegar
- 1/4 cup chopped fresh dill
- salt and ground black pepper to taste
- 1 cucumber, peeled and diced
- 1 cup chopped broccoli
- 1 cup chopped cauliflower
- 2 plum tomatoes, diced
- 1/4 head red cabbage, shredded
- 1/4 large red onion, diced
- 1/2 red bell pepper, chopped
- 1/2 green bell pepper, chopped
- 1 (5 ounce) jar pimento-stuffed green olives, sliced
- 1 (4 ounce) package feta cheese, crumbled

Direction

- In a bowl, whisk together black pepper, salt, dill, vinegar and oil.
- In a large bowl, mix together feta cheese, olives, green bell pepper, red bell pepper, red onion, red cabbage, plum tomatoes, cauliflower, broccoli and cucumber. Add dressing to vegetable mixture and toss until coated. Chill for a minimum of 1 hour until flavors are well marinated.

Nutrition Information

- Calories: 268 calories;
- Total Carbohydrate: 8.4 g
- Cholesterol: 13 mg
- Total Fat: 25.4 g
- Protein: 3.9 g
- Sodium: 538 mg

24. Chicken Dilly

"This dish is a sauté of eggplant and chicken, and then baked with onion, tomato, turmeric, and dill weed. You can enjoy this dish with cooked rice if you want."
Serving: 8 | Prep: 30m | Ready in: 1h30m

Ingredients

- 1 (4 pound) chicken, cut into pieces
- 1 eggplant, sliced into 1/2 inch rounds
- 5 tomatoes, sliced
- 1 onion, thinly sliced
- 2 tablespoons chopped fresh dill weed
- 2 tablespoons ground turmeric
- salt to taste

Direction

- Start preheating the oven to 375°F (190°C).
- Sauté chicken in a big frying pan until it turns brown. Take out of the frying pan and put aside. Sauté eggplant slices in the same frying pan until it turns light brown.
- In a lightly oiled 9x13" baking plate, put the sautéed eggplant and chicken. Put onion and tomato slices on top, and then use salt, turmeric, and dill weed to sprinkle to taste.
- Put in the preheated oven and bake at 375°F (190°C) until the juices run clear and the chicken is thoroughly cooked, about 45 minutes.

Nutrition Information

- Calories: 330 calories;
- Total Carbohydrate: 10 g
- Cholesterol: 97 mg
- Total Fat: 17.6 g
- Protein: 32.4 g
- Sodium: 101 mg

25. Chicken With Sugar Snap Peas & Spring Herbs

"Chicken cutlets with a beautiful sauce made with artichoke hearts and sugar snap peas. Sprouted beans are optional but they really work well in this dish. Try them on a salad if you have some extras."
Serving: 4 | Ready in: 35m

Ingredients

- 1 cup reduced-sodium chicken broth
- 1 teaspoon Dijon mustard
- ½ teaspoon salt
- Freshly ground pepper to taste
- 2 teaspoons plus 1 tablespoon flour, divided
- 1 pound thin-sliced chicken breast cutlets
- 1 tablespoon extra-virgin olive oil
- 8 ounces sugar snap peas, cut in half (2 cups)
- 1 14-ounce can quartered artichoke hearts, rinsed
- ¼ cup sprouted beans, (see Note), optional
- 3 tablespoons minced fresh herbs, such as chives, tarragon or dill
- 2 teaspoons champagne vinegar, or white-wine vinegar

Direction

- In a small mixing bowl, stir together 2 teaspoons flour, pepper, salt, mustard, and broth until no lumps remain.
- Sprinkle the remaining 1 tablespoon flour to coat both sides of the chicken. In a large nonstick skillet, heat oil over medium-high heat. Add chicken and cook in 2 batches for about 2 minutes on each side until golden, adjusting heat to avoid burning if needed. Remove cooked chicken to a plate, cover to keep warm with foil.
- Stir broth mixture into the pan with artichoke hearts, snap peas, and sprouted beans (if using). Bring the mixture to a simmer, stirring continuously. Lower heat to maintain a gentle simmer and cook for 3 to 5 minutes until snap peas are tender-crisp.
- Nestle the chicken into vegetables in the pan and simmer for 1 to 2 minutes until heated

through. Turn off the heat, mix in vinegar and herbs.

Nutrition Information

- Calories: 250 calories;
- Total Carbohydrate: 20 g
- Cholesterol: 63 mg
- Total Fat: 7 g
- Fiber: 10 g
- Protein: 28 g
- Sodium: 571 mg
- Sugar: 3 g
- Saturated Fat: 1 g

26. Chickpea "tuna" Salad Sandwiches

"Mashed chickpeas taste like tuna. Stir it with the usual tuna salad and nori and you will have a tuna sandwich for vegetarians."
Serving: 4 | Prep: 15m | Ready in: 30m

Ingredients

- Chickpea "Tuna" Salad:
- 1/2 sheet nori (dried seaweed), torn into small pieces
- 1 (15 ounce) can no-salt-added chickpeas, drained and rinsed
- 1/4 cup vegan mayonnaise
- 1/3 cup minced or finely grated carrot
- 1/3 cup finely diced celery
- 2 tablespoons dried minced onion
- 2 tablespoons fresh dill
- 1/2 teaspoon salt
- black pepper to taste
- Sandwiches:
- 8 slices whole wheat bread, toasted
- 1/4 cup vegan mayonnaise
- 8 lettuce leaves
- 8 tomato slices

Direction

- In a blender, pulse nori until having a fine powder. Put aside and allow the dust to settle.
- In a big bowl, use a potato masher with small holes (chickpeas will slip through mashers with zigzag or bigger holes) or a sturdy fork to mash chickpeas until mostly crumbled. Make sure to not over mash. The chickpeas should maintain some texture.
- Mix in mayo and mash a bit more. Mix in pepper, salt, dill, onion, celery, carrot, and nori powder. Put a cover on and refrigerate for a minimum of 15 minutes and a maximum of 3 days.
- To prepare sandwiches, generously spread mayo over the toast (approximately 1 1/2 teaspoons each slice). Put between each slice the tomato, lettuce, and salad. Slice the sandwiches into two diagonally.

Nutrition Information

- Calories: 360 calories;
- Total Carbohydrate: 43.6 g
- Cholesterol: 0 mg
- Total Fat: 16 g
- Protein: 11.8 g
- Sodium: 690 mg

27. Chilled Cucumber Yogurt Soup

"This Mediterranean soup is great for a burning summer night. Adjust the amount garlic and lemon to suit your palate. A half of an avocado makes this soup creamier.""
Serving: 4 | Prep: 20m | Ready in: 20m

Ingredients

- 4 small seedless cucumbers - peeled and grated
- 1 tablespoon fresh lemon juice
- 1 bunch fresh mint leaves, chopped
- 1 bunch fresh dill, chopped
- 2 cloves garlic, crushed
- 2 cups plain yogurt

- 1 tablespoon olive oil
- 1 teaspoon salt (optional)
- 1/4 cup raisins (optional)

Direction

- In a large mixing bowl, combine salt, olive oil, yogurt, garlic, dill, mint, lemon juice, and grated cucumber; stir well with a large spoon. Transfer the mixture to a blender and process on high speed until no lumps remain. Serve right away or refrigerate until ready. Pour the soup evenly into 4 serving bowls; add about 1 tablespoon raisins on top of each portion.

Nutrition Information

- Calories: 168 calories;
- Total Carbohydrate: 22.9 g
- Cholesterol: 7 mg
- Total Fat: 5.8 g
- Protein: 8.5 g
- Sodium: 677 mg

28. Chilled Yellow Squash Soup With Dill

"I keep yellow squash skin on for this soup. They add a lovely color to the soup and also make it taste better. You can use zucchini instead, but make sure to choose the seedless and small ones."
Serving: 8 | Prep: 15m | Ready in: 4h45m

Ingredients

- 2 tablespoons olive oil
- 2 pounds yellow summer squash - halved, seeded, and sliced
- 1 onion, chopped
- 2 quarts vegetable broth
- 4 ounces plain yogurt
- salt and pepper to taste
- lemon juice, or to taste (optional)
- 2 tablespoons minced fresh dill

Direction

- In a big saucepan, heat olive oil over medium heat and cook onion for 5 minutes until opaque and tender. Add yellow squash. Stir and cook for 5 minutes until beginning to get tender. Add broth and simmer. Put a cover on, lower the heat, and simmer for 20 minutes until tender.
- Use a stick blender to puree the soup until creamy. Allow cooling to lukewarm. Mix in yogurt and use lemon juice, pepper, and salt to season. Mix in dill and refrigerate for a minimum of 4 hours. Enjoy cold.

Nutrition Information

- Calories: 96 calories;
- Total Carbohydrate: 11.9 g
- Cholesterol: < mg
- Total Fat: 4.4 g
- Protein: 3 g
- Sodium: 493 mg

29. Chilly Dilly Cucumber Soup

"The secret to this dish is that you have to use fresh dill for the yogurt garnish and broth. This dish needs a lot of herbs. If your homegrown herbs are not available; you will need 2-3-ounce packets."
Serving: 5 | Ready in: 3h50m

Ingredients

- 4 cups reduced-sodium chicken broth
- 1½ cups chopped peeled waxy, thin-skinned potatoes (such as red or Yukon Gold, not russets)
- ½ cup chopped cauliflower or ½ cup additional chopped peeled potatoes
- ½ cup chopped celery
- 1 large handful whole fresh dill sprigs (including stems), plus ¼ cup coarsely chopped dill leaves, plus small sprigs for garnish

- 1 handful whole fresh chives, plus ¼ cup coarsely chopped chives, plus more for garnish
- 1 cup low-fat or nonfat plain yogurt
- 1 tablespoon butter
- 1¼ cups finely diced seeded peeled cucumber, plus thin half-moon slices for garnish
- Freshly ground pepper to taste

Direction

- In a big saucepan, mix together celery, cauliflower (or additional potato), potatoes, and broth. Top with whole dill and chives. Boil over medium-high heat. Adjust the heat so that it boils quickly and cook for 15-18 minutes until the vegetables are very soft when using a fork to pierce. Take away from heat and put aside until slightly cooled.
- In a food processor, process yogurt, 1/4 cup chopped chives, and 1/4 cup chopped dill until mixture becomes a bit green and herbs are chopped finely. In a bowl, put half of the mixture; chill in the fridge, covered, to be used later as garnish. Let the rest of the mixture stay in the processor.
- Lift off the herbs in the pan with a fork and throw away. Use a slotted spoon to move the vegetables to the processor (let the broth stay in the pan). Add butter; blend until very smooth, scraping down the sides as necessary.
- Put the diced cucumber in the broth. Boil gently and cook for 3 minutes until the cucumbers are just thoroughly cooked but still slightly crunchy. Take away from heat. Thoroughly mix the pureed vegetables into the cucumber mixture. Use pepper to season. Chill for a minimum of 3 hours and a maximum of 3 days, until cold.
- Enjoy the soup with a dollop of the saved herbed yogurt. Use chopped chives, small sprigs of dill, and/or half-slices of cucumber to garnish if you want.

Nutrition Information

- Calories: 106 calories;
- Total Carbohydrate: 14 g
- Cholesterol: 9 mg
- Total Fat: 3 g
- Fiber: 1 g
- Protein: 6 g
- Sodium: 491 mg
- Sugar: 5 g
- Saturated Fat: 2 g

30. Chive And Dill Muffins

"These savory muffins are the best for the weekend."
Serving: 12 | Prep: 10m | Ready in: 40m

Ingredients

- 1 cup all-purpose flour
- 1 cup yellow cornmeal
- 1 tablespoon white sugar
- 2 teaspoons baking powder
- 1 teaspoon salt
- 1/2 teaspoon baking soda
- 1/2 teaspoon cayenne pepper
- 1/4 cup chopped fresh chives
- 1/4 cup chopped fresh dill
- 1 1/2 cups plain yogurt
- 2 large eggs
- 3 tablespoons butter, melted

Direction

- Start preheating the oven to 425°F (220°C). Oil 12 muffin cups.
- In a bowl, combine cayenne pepper, baking soda, salt, baking powder, sugar, cornmeal, and flour. Mix in dill and chives.
- In another bowl, combine melted butter, eggs, and yogurt; add to the dry ingredients and mix just until combined into a batter.
- Put in each prepared muffin cup 1/3 cup of batter.
- Put in the preheated oven and bake for 20 minutes until they turn golden and a toothpick will come out clean when you stick it in the middle. Let cool in the pan for 10 minutes before taking it out. Enjoy warm.

Nutrition Information

- Calories: 142 calories;
- Total Carbohydrate: 20.7 g
- Cholesterol: 40 mg
- Total Fat: 4.5 g
- Protein: 4.7 g
- Sodium: 382 mg

31. Chorizo Chicken Roll

"Your ordinary chicken breast will taste even better with these spicy flavors."
Serving: 2 | Prep: 10m | Ready in: 33m

Ingredients

- 2 skinless, boneless chicken breast halves - pounded thin
- 1 chorizo sausage, removed from casing
- 1/2 teaspoon dill
- 1/4 cup bread crumbs
- 1/2 ounce pine nuts, chopped
- 1/4 teaspoon salt and freshly ground pepper, to taste
- olive oil for brushing
- 1 1/2 teaspoons olive oil

Direction

- Start preheating the oven to 350°F (175°F). Use vegetable oil cooking spray to spray a glass baking plate.
- On a work surface, put the chicken breasts and evenly spread chorizo over. Drizzle with pine nuts, breadcrumbs, and dill. Roll tightly, use olive oil to brush, and pepper and salt to season. Put in the prepared baking plate with the seam side turning down.
- Put in the preheated oven and bake for 20 minutes until the chicken has thoroughly cooked. Take the chicken out of the oven, and cut into 1" thick slices. In a skillet over medium-high heat, put 1 1/2 teaspoons of olive oil. Put the chicken slices in and fry until turning light brown, about 1-2 minutes each side.

Nutrition Information

- Calories: 431 calories;
- Total Carbohydrate: 11.8 g
- Cholesterol: 98 mg
- Total Fat: 25.5 g
- Protein: 37.2 g
- Sodium: 823 mg

32. Classic Crab And Shrimp Salad

"A salad that pleases anyone who likes seafood."
Serving: 4 | Prep: 25m | Ready in: 25m

Ingredients

- 6 ounces fresh crabmeat, drained and flaked
- 5 ounces small cooked shrimp, chopped
- 1 stalk celery, diced
- 1 green bell pepper, seeded and chopped
- 1 onion, diced
- 3/4 cup mayonnaise
- 2 teaspoons fresh dill, finely chopped
- 1 teaspoon Worcestershire sauce
- salt and ground black pepper to taste

Direction

- In a bowl, put onion, bell pepper, celery, shrimp and crabmeat. Mix Worcestershire sauce, dill and mayonnaise in till blended evenly. Season with pepper and salt to taste. Before serving, refrigerate for an hour.

Nutrition Information

- Calories: 389 calories;
- Total Carbohydrate: 6.5 g
- Cholesterol: 94 mg
- Total Fat: 33.9 g
- Protein: 15.4 g
- Sodium: 434 mg

33. Cool And Creamy Cucumber Salad

"This dish is perfect for a hot summer day. If you don't like onion, you can use sweet bell peppers instead."
Serving: 8 | Prep: 15m | Ready in: 4h15m

Ingredients

- 4 English (seedless) cucumbers, thinly sliced
- 2 green bell peppers, cut into thin matchsticks
- 1 (32 ounce) container plain yogurt
- 1 cup sour cream
- 2 tablespoons apple cider vinegar
- 1/2 cup chopped fresh dill, or more to taste
- 1 tablespoon salt
- 2 teaspoons ground black pepper

Direction

- In a strainer, put bell peppers and cucumbers; let the liquid strain for 4 hours. As the vegetables are straining, put yogurt into a paper towel-lined separate strainer and let sit for 4 hours to let the extra whey strain from the yogurt.
- In a big salad bowl, mix together black pepper, salt, dill, vinegar, sour cream, thickened yogurt, bell peppers, and cucumbers. Refrigerate before enjoying.

Nutrition Information

- Calories: 153 calories;
- Total Carbohydrate: 11.2 g
- Cholesterol: 27 mg
- Total Fat: 9.8 g
- Protein: 6.6 g
- Sodium: 941 mg

34. Corn, Zucchini, And Tomato Pie

"This pie is made with tomatoes, corn, and vegetables. It's tasty and great for the summer."
Serving: 8 | Prep: 25m | Ready in: 1h

Ingredients

- 5 small zucchini, cut into matchsticks
- 3 cups fresh corn kernels
- 2 tablespoons butter, melted
- 2 tablespoons chopped fresh dill, or more to taste
- 2 teaspoons salt
- 1 teaspoon ground black pepper
- 3 tomatoes, cut into thick slices, or more to taste
- 1/2 cup grated Parmesan cheese
- 1/4 cup dry bread crumbs
- 2 tablespoons olive oil

Direction

- Start preheating the oven to 375°F (190°C).
- In a 9x13-inch baking plate, mix together 1/2 teaspoon pepper, 1 teaspoon salt, dill, butter, corn, and zucchini. Mix to blend the vegetables. Use tomato slices to cover. Use the left pepper and salt to sprinkle on top.
- In a small bowl, mix together bread crumbs and Parmesan cheese. Drizzle the tomatoes with this mixture. Sprinkle the top with olive oil.
- Put in the preheated oven and bake without cover for 30 minutes until the vegetables are soft. Take out of the oven and let to sit for 5 minutes. Enjoy.

Nutrition Information

- Calories: 163 calories;
- Total Carbohydrate: 18.5 g
- Cholesterol: 12 mg
- Total Fat: 8.8 g
- Protein: 5.7 g
- Sodium: 723 mg

35. Creamy Dill Dip

"This creamy and tangy dip goes perfectly with different kinds of food such as crackers, vegetables, or potato chips. Prepare this dip a night beforehand for the best flavor.""
Serving: 32

Ingredients

- 1 cup mayonnaise
- 1 cup sour cream
- 1 tablespoon dried dill weed
- 1 tablespoon dried minced onion, rehydrated
- 1 teaspoon Beau Monde ™ seasoning

Direction

- Combine Beau Monde seasoning, onion, dill weed, sour cream, and mayonnaise in a small mixing bowl. Stir until well incorporated. Chill, covered, overnight before serving.

Nutrition Information

- Calories: 65 calories;
- Total Carbohydrate: 0.7 g
- Cholesterol: 6 mg
- Total Fat: 7 g
- Protein: 0.3 g
- Sodium: 43 mg

36. Creamy Dill Dip Ii

"A useful recipe which is for chips, veggies and etc. and mayonnaise free! Can be halve or doubled. Use 1/3 amount of dried dill if you don't have the fresh one."
Serving: 16 | Prep: 5m | Ready in: 5m

Ingredients

- 1 (8 ounce) package cream cheese, at room temperature
- 1 cup sour cream
- 2 tablespoons finely chopped green onions
- 1/2 teaspoon salt
- 2 tablespoons chopped fresh dill weed
- 1/2 teaspoon minced garlic (optional)
- 2 tablespoons milk (optional)

Direction

- Use an electric mixer to blend together the sour cream and cream cheese in a medium bowl until turns to smooth texture. Stir in the garlic, dill, salt, and green onions. Place inside the refrigerator to enhance the flavors for 30 minutes, Stir in milk 1 tablespoon at a time until you achieve the consistency you want if the dip is too thick after chilling.

Nutrition Information

- Calories: 81 calories;
- Total Carbohydrate: 1.2 g
- Cholesterol: 22 mg
- Total Fat: 7.9 g
- Protein: 1.6 g
- Sodium: 123 mg

37. Creamy Dill Dipping Sauce

"This dill dipping sauce is so creamy.""
Serving: 5 | Prep: 1h5m | Ready in: 1h5m

Ingredients

- 1/2 cup sour cream
- 1/4 cup mayonnaise
- 2 tablespoons chopped fresh dill
- 1 teaspoon lemon juice
- salt and pepper to taste

Direction

- Combine pepper, salt, lemon juice, dill, mayonnaise, and sour cream in a small mixing bowl. Chill, covered for 1 to 2 hours before eating.

Nutrition Information

- Calories: 129 calories;
- Total Carbohydrate: 1.5 g

- Cholesterol: 14 mg
- Total Fat: 13.6 g
- Protein: 0.9 g
- Sodium: 76 mg

38. Creamy Dill Sauce

"To reduce fat and calories, you can cut mayonnaise and substitute with yogurt. This sauce is simple and can go with any delicate dish."
Serving: 8 | Ready in: 10m

Ingredients

- ¼ cup reduced-fat mayonnaise
- ¼ cup nonfat plain yogurt
- 2 scallions, thinly sliced
- 1 tablespoon lemon juice
- 1 tablespoon finely chopped fresh dill, or parsley
- Freshly ground pepper, to taste

Direction

- In a small bowl, mix together pepper, dill (or parsley), lemon juice, scallions, yogurt, and mayonnaise, and mix thoroughly.

Nutrition Information

- Calories: 25 calories;
- Total Carbohydrate: 3 g
- Cholesterol: 2 mg
- Total Fat: 1 g
- Fiber: 0 g
- Protein: 1 g
- Sodium: 67 mg
- Sugar: 1 g
- Saturated Fat: 0 g

39. Creamy Herb Dip

"This flavorful dip can be enjoyed with anything."
Serving: 8 | Ready in: 15m

Ingredients

- ¼ cup reduced-fat cream cheese, (Neufchâtel), softened (2 ounces)
- 2 tablespoons buttermilk, or low-fat milk
- 2 tablespoons chopped fresh chives, or scallions
- 1 tablespoon chopped fresh dill, or parsley
- 1 teaspoon prepared horseradish, or more to taste
- Pinch of sugar
- ⅛ teaspoon salt
- Freshly ground pepper, to taste

Direction

- In a small bowl, put cream cheese and mix in buttermilk (or milk) until smooth. Stir in pepper, salt, sugar, horseradish, dill (or parsley), and chives (or scallions).

Nutrition Information

- Calories: 20 calories;
- Total Carbohydrate: 1 g
- Cholesterol: 5 mg
- Total Fat: 2 g
- Fiber: 0 g
- Protein: 1 g
- Sodium: 77 mg
- Sugar: 1 g
- Saturated Fat: 1 g

40. Crispy Cucumbers And Tomatoes In Dill Dressing

""This salad is perfect to enjoy in the summer. It has onion, fresh tomatoes and crispy cucumbers.""
Serving: 6 | Prep: 15m | Ready in: 30m

Ingredients

- 1/4 cup cider vinegar
- 1 teaspoon white sugar
- 1/2 teaspoon salt
- 1/2 teaspoon chopped fresh dill weed
- 1/4 teaspoon ground black pepper
- 2 tablespoons vegetable oil
- 2 cucumbers, sliced
- 1 cup sliced red onion
- 2 ripe tomatoes, cut into wedges

Direction

- Whisk oil, pepper, dill, salt, sugar, and vinegar in a large bowl. Add in tomatoes, onion, and cucumbers. Mix and let sit for 15 minutes at least before serving.

Nutrition Information

- Calories: 71 calories;
- Total Carbohydrate: 6.7 g
- Cholesterol: 0 mg
- Total Fat: 4.7 g
- Protein: 1 g
- Sodium: 199 mg

41. Crispy Tofu And Bacon Wraps

"We need to change the way we think about tofu after trying this recipe.""
Serving: 10 | Prep: 30m | Ready in: 1h

Ingredients

- 1 (16 ounce) package tofu, drained and cubed
- 1 yellow onion, roughly chopped
- 6 large green onions, chopped
- 1 medium red bell pepper, coarsely chopped
- 8 cloves garlic
- 20 mushrooms
- 1 tomato, coarsely chopped
- 3/4 cup crumbled cooked bacon
- 1 tablespoon fish sauce
- 2 tablespoons red wine
- 1/4 cup chopped fresh Italian parsley
- 1/4 teaspoon salt
- 1/2 teaspoon black pepper
- 1/4 teaspoon curry powder
- 1/4 teaspoon mustard powder
- 1/4 teaspoon dill weed
- 1/2 teaspoon ground ginger
- 1 (12 ounce) package egg roll wrappers
- canola oil for frying

Direction

- In the bowl of a processor, combine bacon, tomato, mushrooms, garlic, red pepper, green onion, yellow onion, and tofu. Season with ginger, dill, mustard powder, curry powder, pepper, salt, parsley, red wine, and fish sauce; process the mixture until smooth.
- In a work surface, place an egg roll wrapper with a corner pointing towards you. Ladle 1-2 tablespoons of tofu puree between the center and bottom corner of the wrapper. Fold the closest corner over the filling, then fold the two sides. Moisten the furthest corner with some water and roll up carefully.
- In a large pot, heat a few inches of canola oil to 350°F (175°C). Fry a few tofu wraps at a time until center is cooked and outside turns golden brown. Transfer to paper towels to drain and serve hot.

Nutrition Information

- Calories: 296 calories;
- Total Carbohydrate: 26.7 g
- Cholesterol: 9 mg
- Total Fat: 16 g
- Protein: 12.7 g
- Sodium: 634 mg

42. Crispy Zucchini Fritters

"You can add zucchini into these delicious fritters to make it a vegan main course or serve on the side of your preferred meat. If desired, sprinkle with sour cream."
Serving: 4 | Prep: 25m | Ready in: 31m

Ingredients

- 3 1/3 cups grated zucchini (courgette)
- 6 spring onions, chopped
- 1 bunch fresh dill, chopped
- salt to taste
- 1 egg, beaten
- 2 tablespoons all-purpose flour
- 1 clove garlic, minced
- 2 tablespoons vegetable oil

Direction

- In a large bowl, mix dill, spring onions and zucchini. Mix in salt. Place in egg and stir until combined well. Mix in garlic and flour until the batter comes together.
- Over medium-high heat, heat oil in a large skillet; add tablespoonfuls of the batter in the hot oil. Fry for about 3 minutes on each side until cooked through and browned.

Nutrition Information

- Calories: 120 calories;
- Total Carbohydrate: 9 g
- Cholesterol: 46 mg
- Total Fat: 8.4 g
- Protein: 3.9 g
- Sodium: 75 mg

43. Cucamelon Pickles

"Cucamelons if eaten alone will be very plain, but pickle them and you will have a very delicious pickle. They taste best after day 7 and can last for 1 month in the fridge."
Serving: 8 | Prep: 20m | Ready in: 3days25m

Ingredients

- 2 1/2 cups cucamelons
- 2 green chile peppers, halved and seeded
- 2 sprigs fresh dill
- 1 tablespoon yellow mustard seeds
- 1 tablespoon dill seed
- 2 teaspoons crushed black peppercorns
- 3/4 cup water
- 3/4 cup apple cider vinegar, or more as needed
- 1 tablespoon coarse salt

Direction

- Scan a big jar for any cracks. Put in simmering water until the cucamelons are ready. Use soapy, warm water to rinse an unused, new ring and lid.
- In the sterilized jar, put peppercorns, dill seed, yellow mustard seeds, dill, chile peppers, and cucamelons.
- In a saucepan, mix together salt, vinegar, and water, then boil it. Toss for 1 minute until salt melts. Take away from heat and let cool.
- Add the vinegar mixture to the cucamelons until fully submerged. If you are short on liquid, combine equal amounts of vinegar and water and add to the jar. Seal the jar using the lid and let sit for 3-4 days.

Nutrition Information

- Calories: 24 calories;
- Total Carbohydrate: 3.6 g
- Cholesterol: 0 mg
- Total Fat: 0.6 g
- Protein: 1 g
- Sodium: 724 mg

44. Cucumber And Dill Finger Sandwiches

"These beautiful finger sandwiches are perfect for your afternoon tea. Ideally serve them with creamy goat cheese seasoned with garlic and dill.""

Serving: 4

Ingredients

- 1/2 cup Carapelli Premium 100% Italian Extra Virgin Olive Oil
- 2 cups soft goat cheese
- Zest and juice of 1 lemon
- 1 bunch dill, coarsely chopped
- 1 clove garlic, finely grated
- 8 slices sourdough pullman bread, crusts carefully cut off
- 1 English cucumber, peeled and thinly sliced
- 1 shallot, thinly sliced
- Fresh ground pepper and kosher salt to taste

Direction

- In a large mixing bowl, combine grated garlic, dill, olive oil, lemon zest, lemon juice, and goat cheese. Mix everything together using a rubber spatula.
- Spread 8 pieces of bread evenly with soft cheese mixture. Layer on top of 4 pieces of bread with a thin layer of sliced cucumbers. Drizzle sliced shallot over the cucumbers and put the other piece of bread on top of each sandwich.
- Divide each sandwich into 3 rectangular little tea sandwiches and serve right away.

Nutrition Information

- Calories: 824 calories;
- Total Carbohydrate: 38.5 g
- Cholesterol: 90 mg
- Total Fat: 62.9 g
- Protein: 32 g
- Sodium: 916 mg

45. Cucumber And Dill Pasta Salad

"This refreshingly tasty salad is always requested by my children all year round, may it be during the cold winter or on hot summer days."

Serving: 6 | Prep: 10m | Ready in: 30m

Ingredients

- 2 cups macaroni
- 2 cups cucumber - peeled, seeded and chopped
- 1 cup chopped tomatoes
- 1 cup low-fat sour cream
- 1/2 cup skim milk
- 1 tablespoon chopped fresh dill weed
- 1/2 teaspoon coarse ground black pepper
- 1/2 teaspoon salt
- 1 tablespoon distilled white vinegar

Direction

- Boil salted water and cook pasta until tender but still firm to the bite. Drain and wash in cold water. Transfer the pasta into a large bowl.
- Mix together pepper, salt, vinegar, dill, milk and sour cream in a separate bowl. Set aside the dressing.
- Mix the tomatoes and cucumbers into the pasta. Pour in the dressing and thoroughly mix. Cover and place in a refrigerator for at least 1 hour or preferably overnight. Stir thoroughly right before serving.

Nutrition Information

- Calories: 203 calories;
- Total Carbohydrate: 31.3 g
- Cholesterol: 16 mg
- Total Fat: 5.5 g
- Protein: 7 g
- Sodium: 224 mg

46. Cucumber Slices With Dill

"To get the best flavor in this lovely simple-to-prepare cucumber salad, you need to keep it in the fridge for not less than 2 hours so make sure to take that into account."
Serving: 8 | Prep: 15m | Ready in: 2h15m

Ingredients

- 4 large cucumbers, sliced
- 1 onion, thinly sliced
- 1 tablespoon dried dill weed
- 1 cup white sugar
- 1/2 cup white vinegar
- 1/2 cup water
- 1 teaspoon salt (optional)

Direction

- Mix the onions, dill and cucumbers together in a big serving bowl. Mix the water, sugar, salt and vinegar together in a medium-sized bowl and mix until the sugar has dissolved. Pour the vinegar mixture on top of the cucumber mixture. Cover the bowl and keep it in the fridge for not less than 2 hours prior to serving (the dish becomes a lot more flavorful as you marinate the mixture longer).

Nutrition Information

- Calories: 120 calories;
- Total Carbohydrate: 30 g
- Cholesterol: 0 mg
- Total Fat: 0.3 g
- Protein: 1 g
- Sodium: 295 mg

47. Danish Meatballs With Dill Sauce

"Unique and tasty meatballs."
Serving: 12 | Prep: 35m | Ready in: 1h10m

Ingredients

- 1 pound ground beef
- 1/2 pound ground pork
- 1/2 pound ground veal
- 2 teaspoons salt
- 1/2 teaspoon ground black pepper
- 2 eggs
- 1/3 cup finely chopped onion
- 1/2 cup heavy cream
- 1 cup dry bread crumbs
- 1 cup butter
- 1/4 cup all-purpose flour
- 2 cups chicken broth
- 2 cups sour cream
- 1/4 cup chopped fresh dill

Direction

- Preheat an oven to 190°C/375°F.
- Mix heavy cream, onion, eggs, pepper, salt, veal, pork and beef in big bowl. Form mixture to 1-inch balls with moistened hands; roll balls in breadcrumbs till all balls are coated well. Put on big shallow baking sheet in 1 layer.
- In big saucepan, melt 1/2 cup butter on low heat; mix flour in. Mix in chicken broth slowly; mix till bubbly and thick. Blend fresh dill and sour cream in.
- Melt leftover butter in small saucepan; drizzle on meatballs. In preheated oven, bake meatballs for 35 minutes till browned evenly, occasionally turning.
- Put meatballs in chafing dish; cover with sauce and serve.

Nutrition Information

- Calories: 449 calories;
- Total Carbohydrate: 11.1 g
- Cholesterol: 151 mg
- Total Fat: 37.6 g
- Protein: 16.9 g
- Sodium: 795 mg

48. Deep Fried Dill Pickles

"Try this yummy recipe with different kinds of pickles like pickled peppers or pickled vegetables.""
Serving: 12 | Prep: 10m | Ready in: 20m

Ingredients

- 2 eggs
- 1 cup buttermilk
- 1 tablespoon Worcestershire sauce
- 1/2 teaspoon vinegar-based hot pepper sauce
- 3/4 teaspoon cayenne pepper
- 1/4 teaspoon seasoning salt
- 1/4 teaspoon garlic powder
- 1 cup cornmeal
- 2 1/4 cups all-purpose flour
- 1 teaspoon salt
- 3/4 teaspoon ground black pepper
- 1 (32 ounce) jar dill pickle slices
- 1 cup vegetable oil for deep frying
- salt and pepper to taste

Direction

- Combine garlic powder, seasoning salt, cayenne pepper, hot sauce, Worcestershire sauce, buttermilk, 1/4 cup of flour, and 2 eggs in a large mixing bowl.
- Combine 3/4 teaspoon black pepper, salt, 2 cups flour, and cornmeal in another mixing bowl.
- Heat oil in a pot or deep fryer to 365°F (180°C).
- Submerge drained pickles into milk mixture then dip them into flour mixture to coat. Deep fry coated pickles until golden brown. Transfer to paper towels to drain. Sprinkle with pepper and salt to taste.

Nutrition Information

- Calories: 174 calories;
- Total Carbohydrate: 30.3 g
- Cholesterol: 32 mg
- Total Fat: 3.6 g
- Protein: 5.5 g
- Sodium: 1222 mg

49. Deviled Eggs With A Dill Twist

"Instead of mayo, you can add a little dill, fresh dill, and pickle juice to this dish to make it even tastier. Just finish with paprika and mustard and you will have a nice dish to enjoy."
Serving: 6 | Prep: 10m | Ready in: 35m

Ingredients

- 6 eggs
- 1/4 cup mayonnaise
- 1/2 small red onion, chopped
- 2 tablespoons dill pickle juice
- 2 teaspoons dill pickle relish
- 1 teaspoon chopped fresh dill
- 1 teaspoon prepared yellow mustard
- 1 teaspoon paprika

Direction

- In a saucepan, put eggs and fill with water to cover. Boil then cook for 8 minutes. Take away from heat and let the eggs stay for 15 minutes until the water is lukewarm. Put the eggs under cold running water to cool down and remove the shells. Slice the eggs lengthwise into two. Put the yokes in a bowl.
- Combine egg yolks with mustard, fresh dill, relish, dill pickle juice, red onion, and mayonnaise. Put the mixture evenly in the egg whites. Use paprika to drizzle on top.

Nutrition Information

- Calories: 142 calories;
- Total Carbohydrate: 1.6 g
- Cholesterol: 189 mg
- Total Fat: 12.3 g
- Protein: 6.5 g
- Sodium: 240 mg

50. Dill And Shrimp Salad

"A creamy shrimp and dill salad that would be a great filling for pita bread."
Serving: 8 | Prep: 15m | Ready in: 15m

Ingredients

- 3 pounds cooked shrimp
- 2 lemons, juiced
- 1 lime, juiced
- 2 stalks celery, chopped
- 3 green onions, chopped
- 1 tablespoon chopped fresh dill
- 1 cup mayonnaise
- ground black pepper to taste

Direction

- Mix pepper, mayonnaise, dill, onion, celery, lime juice, lemon juice and shrimp together in a large bowl. Get them well incorporate and place in the fridge to get chilled.

Nutrition Information

- Calories: 378 calories;
- Total Carbohydrate: 5.4 g
- Cholesterol: 342 mg
- Total Fat: 23.8 g
- Protein: 36.4 g
- Sodium: 548 mg

51. Dill Butter

"This dish goes very well with toast, cooked potatoes, and carrots. Adding extra oil will make the dish spreadable and tender."
Serving: 48 | Prep: 5m | Ready in: 5m

Ingredients

- 1 pound butter, softened
- 1 cup vegetable oil
- 2 tablespoons dried dill weed

Direction

- In a mixing bowl, put dill, oil, and butter. Whisk until thoroughly combined. Preserve with a cover in the fridge.

Nutrition Information

- Calories: 108 calories;
- Total Carbohydrate: 0.1 g
- Cholesterol: 20 mg
- Total Fat: 12.2 g
- Protein: 0.1 g
- Sodium: 55 mg

52. Dill Cucumber Salad

"It does take a night to marinate this salad but only 2 hours. It's very tasty but not too sweet."
Serving: 4 | Prep: 10m | Ready in: 2h15m

Ingredients

- 1 cup white vinegar
- 1/2 cup white sugar
- 1/2 cup water
- 1 tablespoon chopped fresh dill
- 2 teaspoons salt
- 2 cucumbers, peeled and thinly sliced
- 1/3 cup sour cream

Direction

- In a saucepan, add salt, dill, water, sugar, and vinegar and boil it until sugar is dissolved. In a big bowl, put the mixture on the cucumbers; mix to combine. Put a cover on and put in a fridge for 2 hours until chilled.
- Strain and dispose of the vinegar mixture and mix sour cream into the cucumbers. Chill until ready to serve.

Nutrition Information

- Calories: 151 calories;
- Total Carbohydrate: 28.4 g
- Cholesterol: 8 mg
- Total Fat: 4.2 g

- Protein: 1.2 g
- Sodium: 1176 mg

53. Dill Dip Iii

"This recipe belongs to my mom. This dip will taste better if you prepare it 1 day in advance."
Serving: 32 | Prep: 5m | Ready in: 8h5m

Ingredients

- 2 cups mayonnaise
- 2 cups sour cream
- 1 tablespoon dried parsley
- 3 tablespoons grated onion
- 3 tablespoons dried dill weed
- 1 1/2 tablespoons seasoning salt

Direction

- Mix salt, dill weed, onion, parsley, sour cream, and mayonnaise together in a medium-sized bowl. Combine all together, put a cover on and chill overnight.

Nutrition Information

- Calories: 131 calories;
- Total Carbohydrate: 1.5 g
- Cholesterol: 12 mg
- Total Fat: 14 g
- Protein: 0.7 g
- Sodium: 216 mg

54. Dill Gazpacho

"A mild and fresh gazpacho dish topped with a sprig of fresh dill."
Serving: 6 | Prep: 25m | Ready in: 1h25m

Ingredients

- 6 medium ripe tomatoes, finely chopped
- 2 cucumbers, peeled and finely chopped
- 1 onion, finely chopped
- 1 green bell pepper, finely chopped
- jalapeno pepper, seeded and minced
- 1 large lemon, juiced
- 1 tablespoon balsamic vinegar
- 2 teaspoons olive oil
- 1 teaspoon kosher salt
- 1/2 teaspoon ground black pepper
- 1/4 cup chopped fresh dill

Direction

- Mix together the jalapeno pepper, bell pepper, onion, cucumber and tomatoes in a big bowl, then season it with pepper, salt, olive oil, balsamic vinegar and lemon juice.
- Puree 1/2 of the mixture in a food processor or blender until it has a smooth consistency. Put it back into the bowl, mix in dill and stir well. Put cover and let it chill in the fridge for a minimum of one hour prior to serving.

Nutrition Information

- Calories: 58 calories;
- Total Carbohydrate: 10.9 g
- Cholesterol: 0 mg
- Total Fat: 2 g
- Protein: 2 g
- Sodium: 330 mg

55. Dill Pickle Dip

"I served this dish at our Easter lunch and everyone loved it. You can enjoy it with crackers or chips."
Serving: 12 | Prep: 15m | Ready in: 1h15m

Ingredients

- 1 (8 ounce) package cream cheese, at room temperature
- 1 cup chopped dill pickles, or more to taste
- 1/4 cup finely chopped sweet onion
- 2 tablespoons pickle juice, or more to taste
- 1 teaspoon dried dill weed
- 1/2 teaspoon kosher salt

- 1 pinch freshly ground black pepper, or to taste

Direction

- In a bowl, use a wooden spoon to whisk cream cheese until creamy. Mix in pepper, salt, dill weed, pickle juice, onion, and dill pickles until evenly distributed. Chill for a minimum of 1 hour. Enjoy.

Nutrition Information

- Calories: 69 calories;
- Total Carbohydrate: 1.4 g
- Cholesterol: 21 mg
- Total Fat: 6.5 g
- Protein: 1.5 g
- Sodium: 288 mg

56. Dill Pickle Sandwich Slices

"This pickle is crisp and will make your ordinary sandwich taste so much better."
Serving: 30

Ingredients

- 2 tablespoons Ball® Mixed Pickling Spice
- 2 1/2 cups cider vinegar
- 2 1/2 cups water
- 1/2 cup granulated sugar
- 1/3 cup Ball® Preserving & Pickling Salt
- 3 bay leaves
- 3 garlic cloves
- 1 1/2 teaspoons mustard seeds
- 3 heads fresh dill
- 8 cups sliced, trimmed pickling cucumbers (1/4-inch slices)
- 1/8 teaspoon Ball® Pickle Crisp® Granulates
- 3 Ball® or Kerr® Pint (16 oz) Jars with lids and bands

Direction

- Prepare jars and canner/ stockpot following the step-by-step instructions.
- Tie a square of cheesecloth around pickling spices, making a spice bag.
- In medium-sized stainless steel saucepan, mix together spice bag, pickling salt, sugar, water, and vinegar. Boil over medium-high heat, tossing to melt salt and sugar. Lower the heat and boil lightly until the liquid has absorbed the spices, about 15 minutes.
- Put in each jar 1 head of dill, 1/2 tsp mustard seeds, 1 garlic clove, and 1 bay leaf. In the hot jars, pack cucumber slices, leaving 1/2 inch above. Add rounded 1/8 tsp Pickle Crisp® Granulates. Spoon hot pickling liquid into the jars, leaving 1/2 inch above. Take out air bubbles, measure the headspace again. Add extra cucumbers to reach the recommended headspace if necessary. Clean the rim, put the lid on the center of the jar. Fasten band until fingertip-tight.
- Put the filled jars in boiling water and process for 15 minutes. Take away the stockpot lid. Wait 5 minutes, and then take out the jars, let cool and preserve.

Nutrition Information

- Calories: 29 calories;
- Total Carbohydrate: 5.2 g
- Cholesterol: 0 mg
- Total Fat: 0.1 g
- Protein: 0.3 g
- Sodium: 1261 mg

57. Dill Poached Salmon

"My family loves this simple poached salmon. You can serve this dish with rice and a veggie."
Serving: 4 | Prep: 5m | Ready in: 20m

Ingredients

- 4 (4 ounce) fillets salmon
- 2 cups chicken stock
- 1 bunch fresh dill tied with kitchen twine

Direction

- In a large pot, put salmon fillets, and then add in chicken stock. Heat to boil, decrease the heat to low and add dill into the pot. Cover the pot and let to cook for about 15 minutes or until the fish flakes easily with a fork.

Nutrition Information

- Calories: 219 calories;
- Total Carbohydrate: 1 g
- Cholesterol: 74 mg
- Total Fat: 10.9 g
- Protein: 25.8 g
- Sodium: 405 mg

58. Dill Sauce For Hamburgers

"This sauce is perfect to enjoy with a hamburger. Every member of my family loves it."
Serving: 6 | Prep: 5m | Ready in: 5m

Ingredients

- 1 cup mayonnaise
- 1 teaspoon Worcestershire sauce
- 2 tablespoons dried dill weed

Direction

- Mix dill weed, Worcestershire sauce, and mayonnaise together in a small bowl; blend thoroughly.

Nutrition Information

- Calories: 267 calories;
- Total Carbohydrate: 1.9 g
- Cholesterol: 14 mg
- Total Fat: 29.2 g
- Protein: 0.5 g
- Sodium: 220 mg

59. Dill Sweet Potato Fries With Vegan Dip

"Make your satisfying meal with this snack.""
Serving: 4 | Prep: 15m | Ready in: 45m

Ingredients

- 1 large sweet potato - peeled, dried, and sliced into fry-size shapes
- 3 tablespoons olive oil
- 1 tablespoon dried dill
- 1/2 teaspoon salt
- 1/4 teaspoon ground mixed peppercorns
- Dipping Sauce:
- 3 tablespoons vegan mayonnaise
- 1 teaspoon dried dill weed
- 1 teaspoon soy sauce

Direction

- Turn oven to 450°F (230°C) to preheat.
- In a mixing bowl, place sweet potato pieces. Add pepper, salt, 1 tablespoon dill, and olive oil; stir until evenly coated. Single layer coated sweet potatoes on a baking sheet, leaving space between each piece.
- Bake for 15 minutes in the preheated oven. Turn fries and keep baking for 15 to 20 minutes until they start to brown.
- In a mixing bowl, combine soy sauce, 1 teaspoon dill, and vegan mayonnaise until incorporated; serve fries with the sauce.

Nutrition Information

- Calories: 242 calories;
- Total Carbohydrate: 25.3 g
- Cholesterol: 0 mg
- Total Fat: 15.3 g
- Protein: 2.1 g
- Sodium: 468 mg

60. Dill, Feta And Garlic Cream Cheese Spread

"This amazing dip is a must-have at any gatherings. You can enjoy it with crackers or raw veggies."
Serving: 24 | Prep: 15m | Ready in: 4h15m

Ingredients

- 2 (8 ounce) packages cream cheese, softened
- 1 (8 ounce) package feta cheese, crumbled
- 3 cloves garlic, peeled and minced
- 2 tablespoons chopped fresh dill

Direction

- Use an electric mixer to blend thoroughly dill, garlic, feta cheese, and cream cheese in a medium-sized bowl. Put a cover on and chill for a minimum of 4 hours.

Nutrition Information

- Calories: 91 calories;
- Total Carbohydrate: 1 g
- Cholesterol: 29 mg
- Total Fat: 8.5 g
- Protein: 2.8 g
- Sodium: 161 mg

61. Dill-infused Deviled Eggs With Bacon Crumble

""Deviled eggs with a new twist!""
Serving: 6 | Prep: 20m | Ready in: 45m

Ingredients

- 6 eggs
- 1 slice bacon
- 2 tablespoons mayonnaise
- 1 tablespoon finely chopped dill
- 1 teaspoon honey mustard
- 1 teaspoon white vinegar
- 1/4 teaspoon salt
- 1 pinch ground black pepper
- 1 pinch paprika

Direction

- Fill water in a large pot and bring to a boil. Add eggs in; allow to cook for 10 minutes. Remove to a bowl and rinse with cold running water till cool down enough to handle. Remove eggshells in the bowl with water.
- In a large skillet, cook bacon over medium-high heat for about 10 minutes till turns browned evenly, occasionally turning. Lay on paper towels to strain; crumble into small pieces.
- Slice eggs in half lengthways and remove yolks to a bowl. Use a folk to mash yolks. Add pepper, salt, white vinegar, honey mustard, dill, and mayonnaise in; whisk till smooth.
- Fill in the egg whites with yolk mixture. Use paprika and bacon crumbles for garnish.

Nutrition Information

- Calories: 116 calories;
- Total Carbohydrate: 1.2 g
- Cholesterol: 189 mg
- Total Fat: 9.3 g
- Protein: 7 g
- Sodium: 235 mg

62. Dill-tarragon Salmon

"This salmon dish is tasty and very easy to make."
Serving: 4 | Prep: 10m | Ready in: 25m

Ingredients

- 1/2 cup plain yogurt
- 1 tablespoon mayonnaise
- 1/4 teaspoon lemon juice
- 1 teaspoon dried tarragon
- 1 teaspoon dried dill
- 3/4 cup shredded mozzarella cheese
- 1 tablespoon grated Parmesan cheese, optional
- 4 (4 ounce) salmon fillets, skin removed

Direction

- Start preheating the oven to 400°F (200°). Use nonstick cooking spray to spray a glass baking plate.
- In a small bowl, combine Parmesan, mozzarella, dill, tarragon, lemon juice, mayonnaise, and yogurt. In the oil-coated baking plate, put the fish fillets, and use the cheese mixture to spread evenly.
- Put in the preheated oven and bake for 15 minutes until a fork can easily flake the fish.

Nutrition Information

- Calories: 313 calories;
- Total Carbohydrate: 3.3 g
- Cholesterol: 85 mg
- Total Fat: 19.3 g
- Protein: 30 g
- Sodium: 259 mg

63. Dilled Creamed Potatoes

"My mother-in-law gave me this recipe. It has become a tradition at our family get together parties. You can use either peeled or cubed potatoes instead of baby potatoes.""
Serving: 10 | Prep: 15m | Ready in: 50m

Ingredients

- 2 pounds new potatoes
- 2 tablespoons olive oil
- 1 small onion, diced
- 3 cloves garlic, minced
- 1 quart heavy cream
- 1 cup chopped fresh dill
- salt and pepper to taste

Direction

- Pour water into a large pot to cover potatoes. Bring to a boil, and cook until softened, about 15 minutes.
- In a skillet, heat olive oil over medium heat, add garlic and onion and stir-fry until tender.
- Drain potatoes and put them back to the pot. Pour cream into the pot, and stir in dill, garlic, and onion. Bing the mixture to a boil, turn heat down to low, and simmer, stirring occasionally, for 20 minutes until thickened. Add pepper and salt to taste.

Nutrition Information

- Calories: 429 calories;
- Total Carbohydrate: 20.3 g
- Cholesterol: 130 mg
- Total Fat: 38.1 g
- Protein: 3.7 g
- Sodium: 42 mg

64. Dilled Garlic

"This pickled garlic recipe can be made as hot as you want it to be. Begin with 1/4 teaspoon cayenne pepper, then increase until your limit of taste is reached."
Serving: 64 | Prep: 1h | Ready in: 1h15m

Ingredients

- 2 pounds garlic, peeled
- 1 sprig chopped fresh dill
- cayenne pepper to taste
- 4 1/2 cups distilled white vinegar
- 4 tablespoons salt

Direction

- Fill cayenne pepper, chopped fresh dill, and garlic in sterile containers to within 1 inch of the top.
- In a medium saucepan, combine salt and distilled white vinegar, and bring to a boil.
- Transfer the hot distilled vinegar and salt mixture to the garlic mixture in the containers. Fill to about 1/4 inch from the container surface. Chill, sealed, in the fridge before using.

Nutrition Information

- Calories: 21 calories;

- Total Carbohydrate: 4.7 g
- Cholesterol: 0 mg
- Total Fat: 0.1 g
- Protein: 0.9 g
- Sodium: 438 mg

65. Dilled Green Beans

"A great side dish with beans.""
Serving: 5

Ingredients

- 2 quarts water
- 2 pounds fresh green beans, washed and trimmed
- 1 teaspoon salt
- 2 teaspoons mustard seed
- 2 teaspoons dried dill weed
- 1 teaspoon red pepper flakes
- 1 teaspoon dill seed
- 4 cloves garlic, minced
- 2 cups distilled white vinegar
- 2/3 cup white sugar
- 2 cups water

Direction

- Boil 2 quarts of water. Pour in green beans and boil just until tender, about 5 minutes. Lightly soak the beans in cold water to maintain color, drain thoroughly.
- Combine garlic, dill seed, chiles, dill weed, mustard seed, and salt in a large mixing bowl, mix well. Stir in cooled beans.
- Bring 2 cups water, vinegar, salt, and sugar (to taste) in a small saucepan to a boil. Pour over beans and spice mixture. Stir to combine.
- Transfer the mixture into an airtight container and put into the fridge to chill at least overnight before serving. Keeping beans marinated 1-week in advance in refrigerator gives the best flavor.

Nutrition Information

- Calories: 176 calories;
- Total Carbohydrate: 41.7 g
- Cholesterol: 0 mg
- Total Fat: 0.8 g
- Protein: 4 g
- Sodium: 489 mg

66. Dilly Beans

"This is an old-style recipe of spicy pickled green beans that was made by my grandmother.""
Serving: 32 | Prep: 30m | Ready in: 35m

Ingredients

- 6 cups water
- 1 cup pickling salt
- 6 cups distilled white vinegar
- 8 heads fresh dill weed
- 1/2 cup pickling spice
- 1/2 cup mustard seed
- 8 dried red chile peppers
- 16 cloves garlic, peeled
- 1 teaspoon alum
- 5 pounds fresh green beans, rinsed and trimmed

Direction

- Steep 8 (1pint) jars in boiling water for at least 5 minutes to sterilize.
- Mix together vinegar, pickling salt, and water in a large pot and bring to a boil. When mixture starts to boil, turn heat down to low, and keep simmering while you pack the jars.
- Place 1/8 teaspoon of alum, 2 cloves of garlic, 1 dried chile pepper, 1 tablespoon of mustard seed, 1 tablespoon of pickling spice, and 1 head of dill in each jar. Place beans in a standing position into the spiced jars.
- Spoon the hot brine into jars, spacing about 1/2 inch from the top. Twist the lids onto the jars, and place jars in hot water bath for 6

minutes to finish the canning process. Store jars for a minimum of 2 weeks before using.

Nutrition Information

- Calories: 42 calories;
- Total Carbohydrate: 7.2 g
- Cholesterol: 0 mg
- Total Fat: 0.9 g
- Protein: 2.1 g
- Sodium: 3481 mg

67. Dilly Cheese Wheat Bread

"You can make a perfect bread machine with this recipe. The dill cheese tastes best when toasted and makes amazing salad croutons."
Serving: 12 | Prep: 10m | Ready in: 10m

Ingredients

- 2/3 cup milk
- 1/2 cup hot water
- 1 teaspoon salt
- 1 tablespoon sugar
- 1 tablespoon dried dill weed
- 1 cup whole wheat flour
- 2 cups bread flour
- 2 teaspoons bread machine yeast
- 1/2 cup grated Cheddar cheese
- 1/2 cup grated Asiago or Parmesan cheese

Direction

- In the bread machine's pan, put the ingredients in the order as the manufacturer recommends. Choose the white bread light crust setting, press Start. If your machine has a Fruit setting, add Asiago and Cheddar cheeses approximately 5 minutes before the kneading cycle has completed, or at the signal.

Nutrition Information

- Calories: 169 calories;
- Total Carbohydrate: 26 g
- Cholesterol: 11 mg

- Total Fat: 4.1 g
- Protein: 7.4 g
- Sodium: 292 mg

68. Dilly Round Steak

"An amazing twist of beef stroganoff. Steaks melt in your mouth with blended flavor from the dill. Interestingly enough, it's super easy to make. Enjoy with noodles or mashed potatoes is also great.""
Serving: 6 | Prep: 15m | Ready in: 6h25m

Ingredients

- 2 pounds boneless round steak, cut into 6 pieces
- salt and ground black pepper to taste
- 1 onion, sliced
- 1/2 cup water
- 1 cube beef bouillon
- 1 teaspoon dill weed
- 1/4 cup cold water
- 1/4 cup all-purpose flour
- 3 tablespoons sour cream, or more to taste

Direction

- Place steaks seasoned with pepper and salt in a slow cooker; add dill, bouillon, 1/2 cup water, and onion.
- Cook on low setting for about 6 hours until steaks are tender. Take steaks out and place them on a serving platter.
- In a mixing bowl, whisk flour and 1/4 cup cold water together until no lumps remain; pour flour mixture into broth mixture in the slow cooker.
- Turn the slow cooker to high heat and cook for about 10 minutes until gravy is thickened. Mix in sour cream, serve with steaks.

Nutrition Information

- Calories: 273 calories;
- Total Carbohydrate: 8 g
- Cholesterol: 84 mg
- Total Fat: 11.9 g

- Protein: 31.6 g
- Sodium: 191 mg

69. Dilly Rye Boat Dip

"This dip is very classic. You can serve this dish at any gatherings or parties. You can use chipped beef instead of corned beef, as well as add more celery salt."
Serving: 10 | Prep: 20m | Ready in: 1h20m

Ingredients

- 1 (1 pound) loaf round rye bread
- 1 cup sour cream
- 1 cup mayonnaise
- 1 (4 ounce) jar dried chipped beef, chopped
- 1 teaspoon Beau Monde ™ seasoning
- 2 teaspoons celery salt
- 3 tablespoons dried dill weed

Direction

- Cut off the 'crown' of the bread with a bread knife. Scoop out the inside of the loaf, and slice into bite-sized cubes for dipping.
- Combine dill weed, celery salt, Beau Monde seasoning, chipped beef, mayonnaise, and sour cream in a medium-sized bowl. Blend well, put a cover on and refrigerate for a minimum of 1 hour.
- Ladle the chilled dip into the emptied bread loaf, and enjoy with cubed bread for dipping.

Nutrition Information

- Calories: 227 calories;
- Total Carbohydrate: 2.6 g
- Cholesterol: 27 mg
- Total Fat: 22.6 g
- Protein: 4.6 g
- Sodium: 749 mg

70. Dilly Tomato And Beet Salad

"It's such a refreshing salad for a warm summer evening with the combination of beets, tomatoes and fresh dill."
Serving: 4 | Prep: 15m | Ready in: 15m

Ingredients

- 1/4 cup safflower oil
- 2 tablespoons walnut oil
- 2 tablespoons olive oil
- 2 tablespoons red wine vinegar
- 1 tablespoon lemon juice
- 1/4 cup minced fresh dill weed
- salt and pepper to taste
- 2 tomatoes, diced
- 1 stalk celery, chopped
- 1 green onion, chopped
- 1 (15 ounce) can red beets, drained and chopped

Direction

- Whisk dill, lemon juice, red wine vinegar, olive oil, walnut oil and safflower oil together in a bowl. Season with pepper and salt.
- Toss together beets, green onion, celery and tomatoes in another bowl, then toss with the dressing mixture right before serving.

Nutrition Information

- Calories: 280 calories;
- Total Carbohydrate: 9.5 g
- Cholesterol: 0 mg
- Total Fat: 27.3 g
- Protein: 1.1 g
- Sodium: 306 mg

71. Dilly-of-a-baked Potato Salad

"Bake and enjoy this potato salad like a potato casserole."
Serving: 4 | Prep: 15m | Ready in: 1h

Ingredients

- 3 russet potatoes

- 2 tablespoons vegetable oil
- 1/2 cup chopped onion
- 2 tablespoons all-purpose flour
- 1 teaspoon prepared mustard
- 1/4 teaspoon celery seed
- 1/3 teaspoon salt
- 1/2 cup water
- 2 tablespoons cider vinegar
- 1/2 cup chopped green bell pepper
- 1/4 cup shredded carrots
- 1/2 teaspoon chopped fresh dill weed
- 1/4 cup grated Parmesan cheese for topping

Direction

- Start preheating the oven to 350°F (175°C).
- Boil a big pot of salted water. Put potatoes and cook for 15-20 minutes until softened but still firm. Strain and let cool. Take the skin off the potatoes and cut 1/4-inch thick, put aside.
- In a medium-sized frying pan, heat oil; sauté onion until tender. Mix in salt, celery seed, mustard, and flour; slowly add vinegar and water, cook over low heat, whisking nonstop until the mixture is thick and boiling.
- Mix dill, carrots, green pepper, and potatoes together in a mixing bowl, add sauce and mix thoroughly. Put half of the mixture on a shallow 8x8-inch baking dish and use half of the cheese to drizzle. Use the rest of the cheese and potato mixture to cover.
- Bake without a cover at 350°F (175°C) until cheese is melted and vegetables are cooked through, about 15-20 minutes

Nutrition Information

- Calories: 236 calories;
- Total Carbohydrate: 34.6 g
- Cholesterol: 4 mg
- Total Fat: 8.6 g
- Protein: 6 g
- Sodium: 287 mg

72. Easy Dill Hollandaise Sauce

"To lessen the preparation time and the mess immensely, in place of a double boiler, microwave has been used to make this hollandaise. The hot melted better gives right heat for the sauce to be cooked. This recipe produces sauce good enough for 2 portions of eggs Benedict.""
Serving: 2 | Prep: 10m | Ready in: 13m

Ingredients

- 1/4 cup unsalted butter
- 1 tablespoon lemon juice
- 1 pinch salt
- 1/2 teaspoon chopped fresh dill
- 3 egg yolks
- 1 tablespoon boiling water

Direction

- In a microwave-safe glass container or a ceramic bowl, melt some butter in the microwave, giving 15 seconds in between to stir to not cause popping, do this for around 1 to 2 minutes. In the melted butter, mix in dill, salt and lemon juice, put back in the microwave for 10 more seconds to cook. In the butter mixture, beat egg yolks strongly for about 30 seconds until smooth. Little by little add in boiling water until smooth and creamy, an additional 1 minute.

Nutrition Information

- Calories: 284 calories;
- Total Carbohydrate: 1.6 g
- Cholesterol: 368 mg
- Total Fat: 29.6 g
- Protein: 4.2 g
- Sodium: 93 mg

73. Easy Lemony-dilly Cucumber Salad

"The combination of cucumber with sugar, dill and lemon zest is perfect for the summer. Eat right away because it cannot be kept well."
Serving: 4 | Prep: 15m | Ready in: 25m

Ingredients

- 1 lemon, zested and juiced
- 2 tablespoons dried dill weed
- 1 teaspoon white sugar
- 1/4 cup mayonnaise
- 2 large English cucumbers, peeled and diced

Direction

- In a bowl, combine sugar, dill, lemon juice and lemon zest together; whisk to dissolve to the sugar. Add mayonnaise and stir until smoothens. Add cucumber and stir with folding method. Set aside for 10 minutes until ready to serve.

Nutrition Information

- Calories: 133 calories;
- Total Carbohydrate: 10.4 g
- Cholesterol: 5 mg
- Total Fat: 11.2 g
- Protein: 1.7 g
- Sodium: 85 mg

74. Easy Potato Salad With Dill

"Add cucumbers to get more crunch in this simple dill potato salad. The dish goes great with apple cider vinegar."
Serving: 5 | Prep: 18m | Ready in: 2h30m

Ingredients

- 1 pound red potatoes, cut into 3/4-inch cubes
- 1/4 cup mayonnaise
- 2 tablespoons cider vinegar
- 2 sprigs chopped fresh dill, or to taste
- salt and pepper to taste
- 1/2 cucumber - peeled, seeded, and finely chopped
- 4 green onions, sliced

Direction

- Cover potatoes with salted water in a large pot. Boil over high heat then lower to medium-low heat. Cover then simmer for 12 minutes till tender. Drain and let steam dry while making the dressing.
- Whisk together pepper, salt, dill, apple cider vinegar and mayonnaise. Add in green onions and cucumber then stir. Gently toss warm potatoes with the dressing till the potatoes are coated. Store in the fridge, covered, for at least 2 hours then serve.

Nutrition Information

- Calories: 150 calories;
- Total Carbohydrate: 16.2 g
- Cholesterol: 4 mg
- Total Fat: 8.9 g
- Protein: 2.2 g
- Sodium: 71 mg

75. Easy Roasted Potatoes

"This is a great and easy recipe for roasted potatoes.""
Serving: 6 | Prep: 15m | Ready in: 55m

Ingredients

- 1 teaspoon McCormick® Dill Weed
- 1 teaspoon McCormick® Garlic Powder
- 1/2 teaspoon salt
- 1/4 teaspoon McCormick® Black Pepper, Coarse Ground
- 2 pounds red potatoes, cut into wedges
- 1 tablespoon olive oil

Direction

- Turn oven to 400°F to preheat. Combine pepper, salt, garlic powder, and dill weed in a small mixing bowl and put to one side.

- In a large mixing bowl, toss potatoes with oil until combined. Sprinkle with seasoning mixture and toss until evenly coated.
- Single layer seasoned potatoes on a 15x10x1-inch baking pan lined with foil.
- Bake in the preheated oven for 40 minutes until the potatoes are golden brown and tender.

Nutrition Information

- Calories: 128 calories;
- Total Carbohydrate: 24.6 g
- Cholesterol: 0 mg
- Total Fat: 2.5 g
- Protein: 3 g
- Sodium: 203 mg

76. Fermented Kosher-style Dill Pickles

"These classic pickles are made without any vinegar, but fully by fermentation. You can make a half-gallon Mason jar of pickles with this recipe. You can add Chile de arbol peppers if you want."
Serving: 16 | Prep: 15m | Ready in: 3days20m

Ingredients

- 1/2 gallon water
- 2 pounds Kirby cucumbers
- 1 cup tap water
- 1/3 cup kosher salt
- 5 cloves fresh garlic, or more to taste
- 1 bunch fresh dill, stems trimmed
- 3 dried chile de arbol peppers (optional)

Direction

- In a pot or a big container, add 1/2 gallon of water. Barely cover and let sit until the dissolved chlorine releases, about 24 hours.
- Bath the cucumbers in ice-cold water or preserve in the fridge to make the cucumbers crunchy, about 1 hour.
- In a saucepan, boil 1 cup of water. Add salt and toss to blend. Put aside to cool.
- Use cold water to rinse the cucumbers and clean any blossoms that may stick to them. Cut big cucumbers lengthwise into 4. Halve lengthwise the medium cucumbers. Keep gherkin-sized cucumbers intact.
- Peel and lightly crush garlic cloves, make sure to not mash them into fragments.
- In a 1/2-gallon Mason jar, add cooled saltwater. Add dried chile peppers, dill, garlic, and cucumbers; sort them decoratively. Pack the cucumbers snugly as they will shrink while they pickle. Add the dechlorinated water to the jar until just covering the cucumbers to prevent the brine from overly diluting.
- Put the lid on the jar loosely and put aside at room temperature. If the jar is too full, put on a plate to collect any dribbles. Let the pickles start fermenting for 12-24 hours. Chill them in the brine with a loose cover while they reach the pickling stage you want: sour, half-sour, or new. Make sure to not overshoot the mark as the refrigeration only slows the fermentation, not stop it.

Nutrition Information

- Calories: 29 calories;
- Total Carbohydrate: 5.5 g
- Cholesterol: 0 mg
- Total Fat: 0.1 g
- Protein: 1.2 g
- Sodium: 1906 mg

77. Feta & Herb Dip

"This tasty white bean dip is loaded with freshly chopped herbs. You can enjoy this dish with any kinds of vegetables you like, such as cauliflower florets, broccoli, snow peas, radishes, bell pepper strips, or baby carrots."
Serving: 8 | Ready in: 30m

Ingredients

- 1 15-ounce can white beans, rinsed
- ¾ cup nonfat plain yogurt
- ½ cup crumbled feta cheese
- 1 tablespoon lemon juice
- 1 teaspoon garlic salt
- 1 teaspoon freshly ground pepper
- ¼ cup chopped fresh parsley
- ¼ cup chopped fresh dill
- ¼ cup chopped fresh mint
- ¼ cup chopped fresh chives

Direction

- Puree pepper, garlic salt, lemon juice, feta, yogurt, and beans in a food processor until smooth. Add herbs; puree until blended. Refrigerate until ready to enjoy.

Nutrition Information

- Calories: 68 calories;
- Total Carbohydrate: 9 g
- Cholesterol: 9 mg
- Total Fat: 2 g
- Fiber: 2 g
- Protein: 5 g
- Sodium: 322 mg
- Sugar: 3 g
- Saturated Fat: 1 g

78. Fish Baked En Croute De Sel (Fish Baked In A Salt Crust)

"Use fish without big scales like salmon, char or trout for the best results."
Serving: 4 | Prep: 30m | Ready in: 1h

Ingredients

- 2 pounds salt
- 7 bay leaves
- 2 pounds whole rainbow trout, gutted and cleaned, heads and tails still on
- 2 sprigs fresh cilantro, or more to taste
- 2 sprigs fresh parsley, or more to taste
- 2 sprigs fresh dill, or more to taste

Direction

- Preheat the oven to 200 degrees C/400 degrees F. Line aluminum foil on a baking sheet.
- Spread 1/4 - 1/2-lb. salt on aluminum foil to around the same shape as the fish. Put bay leaves on salt. Put fish on top. Stuff dill, parsley and cilantro into fish cavity. Firmly pack down leftover salt on fish. Leave tail and head exposed.
- Bake in preheated oven for 30 minutes until salt crust becomes golden.
- Remove fish from oven. Crack open salt crust carefully. Remove the top. Peel off fish skin to expose flesh. Use a spatula/fish knife to lift top fillet off the bones. In one piece, remove bones by lifting from the tail then pull upwards towards the head. Lift bottom fillet out with a spatula/knife.

Nutrition Information

- Calories: 272 calories;
- Total Carbohydrate: 1.1 g
- Cholesterol: 122 mg
- Total Fat: 10.5 g
- Protein: 41.1 g
- Sodium: 88088 mg

79. Fresh Dill Pasta Salad

"A nice variation of your standard shrimp salad"
Serving: 12 | Prep: 10m | Ready in: 2h20m

Ingredients

- 1 (8 ounce) package seashell pasta
- 1 cup mayonnaise
- 1/4 cup sour cream
- 1 1/2 tablespoons lemon juice
- 1 1/2 tablespoons Dijon mustard
- 1/4 cup chopped fresh dill weed
- 1/4 teaspoon ground black pepper
- 2 (4 ounce) cans small shrimp, drained
- 1/2 cup chopped celery
- 1/2 cup chopped seeded cucumber
- 2 tomatoes, diced
- 3 tablespoons minced shallot
- salt to taste

Direction

- Bring lightly salted water to a boil in a large pot. Add pasta and cook for about 8 minutes until tender. Drain and run under cold water until cooled.
- Combine black pepper, dill, mustard, lemon juice, sour cream and mayonnaise in a serving bowl. Gently stir in shallots, tomato, cucumber, celery, shrimp and pasta. Add salt to taste and chill for a minimum of 2 hours before serving.

Nutrition Information

- Calories: 241 calories;
- Total Carbohydrate: 16.8 g
- Cholesterol: 41 mg
- Total Fat: 16.4 g
- Protein: 7.5 g
- Sodium: 192 mg

80. Fresh Herb & Lemon Bulgur Pilaf

"This dish has a rich and bright flavor that comes from lemon, ginger, parsley, mint, and fresh dill."
Serving: 6 | Ready in: 50m

Ingredients

- 2 tablespoons extra-virgin olive oil
- 2 cups chopped onion
- 1 clove garlic, finely chopped
- 1½ cups bulgur, preferably medium or coarse (see Note)
- ½ teaspoon ground turmeric
- ½ teaspoon ground cumin
- 2 cups vegetable broth, or reduced-sodium chicken broth
- 1½ cups chopped carrot
- 2 teaspoons grated or finely chopped fresh ginger
- 1 teaspoon coarse salt
- ¼ cup lightly packed finely chopped fresh dill
- ¼ cup lightly packed finely chopped fresh mint
- ¼ cup lightly packed finely chopped flat-leaf parsley
- 3 tablespoons lemon juice, or more to taste
- ½ cup chopped walnuts, toasted (see Tip)

Direction

- In a broad shallow saucepan or a big high-sided frying pan with a tight-fitting cover, heat oil over medium heat until heated enough to frizzle an onion piece. Add onion, lower the heat to medium-low, cook and toss frequently for 12-18 minutes until it turns golden brown. Mix in garlic and cook, tossing, for 1 minute. Add cumin, turmeric, and bulgur and cook, tossing, for 1 minute until the oil coats the bulgur.
- Add salt, ginger, carrot, and broth; boil it, tossing. Put the cover on and cook over medium-low heat for 15 minutes until the broth incorporates and indentations or "eyes" appear on the bulgur's surface. (Make sure to

not toss the pilaf). Take away from heat and let sit with a cover for 5 minutes.
- Mix lemon juice, parsley, mint, and dill into the pilaf. Put walnuts on top and enjoy.

Nutrition Information

- Calories: 273 calories;
- Total Carbohydrate: 39 g
- Cholesterol: 0 mg
- Total Fat: 12 g
- Fiber: 8 g
- Protein: 7 g
- Sodium: 567 mg
- Sugar: 5 g
- Saturated Fat: 1 g

81. Garbanzo Bean Salad Ii

"This salad is so versatile with many kinds of vegetables, spices and dressing you can add in. By the way, it's an effective way to use up a can of garbanzo beans with just a couple spoonfuls of tomato sauce."
Serving: 4 | Prep: 10m | Ready in: 10m

Ingredients

- 1 (15 ounce) can garbanzo beans, drained and rinsed
- 5 tablespoons tomato sauce
- 1 cup sliced celery
- 1 clove garlic, minced
- 1/2 small onion, thinly sliced
- 1/2 small onion, diced
- 3 tablespoons distilled white vinegar
- 1 tablespoon dill
- ground black pepper to taste

Direction

- Toss together the pepper, dill, distilled white vinegar, diced onion, sliced onion, garlic, celery, tomato sauce and beans gently in a bowl.

Nutrition Information

- Calories: 104 calories;
- Total Carbohydrate: 20.3 g
- Cholesterol: 0 mg
- Total Fat: 0.9 g
- Protein: 4.4 g
- Sodium: 338 mg

82. Garden Fresh Salad

"A perfect summer salad."
Serving: 12 | Prep: 15m | Ready in: 30m

Ingredients

- 1 pound new red potatoes, scrubbed and halved
- 1 pound new white potatoes, scrubbed and halved
- 1/2 pound fresh green beans, trimmed and snapped
- 1/2 pound fresh wax beans, trimmed and snapped
- 1/2 cup mayonnaise
- 2 teaspoons Dijon mustard
- 2 stalks celery, chopped
- 1/3 cup chopped fresh dill
- salt and pepper to taste

Direction

- Cover potatoes with water in a big pot. Boil and cook potatoes for 10 minutes until tender. Add wax beans and green beans at the final 2 minutes to blanch. Drain then rinse with cold water to stop cooking process. Cool then add to the dressing.
- Mix pepper, salt, dill, celery, mustard, and mayonnaise in a big bowl. Add beans and cooled potatoes. Stir until coated. Keep in fridge until serving time.

Nutrition Information

- Calories: 163 calories;
- Total Carbohydrate: 22.5 g

- Cholesterol: 3 mg
- Total Fat: 7.4 g
- Protein: 2.9 g
- Sodium: 86 mg

83. Garlic And Dill Salmon

"This baked salmon is marinated in olive oil, garlic, and dill. This dish is easy to make and it tastes delicious."
Serving: 9 | Prep: 20m | Ready in: 2h35m

Ingredients

- 2 (1.5 pound) salmon fillets
- 1 head garlic, peeled
- 1 ounce fresh dill, chopped
- 1/2 cup olive oil
- 1 teaspoon salt and pepper to taste

Direction

- Blend garlic in a food processor until having a rough mince, add olive oil and dill and pulse several times to blend.
- In a cookie sheet, put the fish fillets with the skin side turning down. Rub on the fish the garlic mixture. Chill for 2 hours.
- Start preheating the oven to 375°F (190°C).
- Put in the preheated oven and bake for 15 minutes. Make sure to not overcook.

Nutrition Information

- Calories: 329 calories;
- Total Carbohydrate: 2.3 g
- Cholesterol: 83 mg
- Total Fat: 21.5 g
- Protein: 30.2 g
- Sodium: 327 mg

84. Garlic Dill Burgers

"The combo of dill and garlic makes a savory burger."
Serving: 4 | Prep: 10m | Ready in: 25m

Ingredients

- 1 1/4 pounds ground beef
- 3 tablespoons ketchup
- 3 tablespoons garlic powder
- 3 tablespoons dried dill
- 2 tablespoons finely chopped dill pickles
- 2 teaspoons mustard

Direction

- Preheat an outdoor grill for moderate-high heat and slightly oil the grate.
- Mix ground beef, pickles, ketchup, dill, mustard and garlic powder in a bowl with your hands; shape into patties.
- Cook patties on the grill until desired doneness is achieved, 7-8 minutes on each side. An instant-read thermometer inserted into the middle registers 70 ° c (160 ° F).

Nutrition Information

- Calories: 339 calories;
- Total Carbohydrate: 9 g
- Cholesterol: 87 mg
- Total Fat: 22.3 g
- Protein: 25.2 g
- Sodium: 301 mg

85. Garlic Dill New Potatoes

"Garlic, butter, and dill make this potato recipe a wonderful side dish.""
Serving: 5 | Prep: 10m | Ready in: 20m

Ingredients

- 8 medium red potatoes, cubed
- 3 tablespoons butter, melted
- 1 tablespoon chopped fresh dill
- 2 teaspoons minced garlic

- 1/4 teaspoon salt

Direction

- Place a steamer basket which contains potatoes in a pan over 1 inch of boiling water. Put a lid on and steam until potatoes are softened but not mushy, about 10 minutes.
- Combine salt, garlic, dill, and butter in a small mixing bowl. Remove cooked potatoes to a serving bowl, and drizzle seasoned butter over them. Toss gradually until evenly coated.

Nutrition Information

- Calories: 330 calories;
- Total Carbohydrate: 62.1 g
- Cholesterol: 18 mg
- Total Fat: 7.2 g
- Protein: 5.9 g
- Sodium: 178 mg

86. George's Salmon-pepper Pate

"You can use your leftover salmon to make this tasty pate."
Serving: 4 | Prep: 10m | Ready in: 1h15m

Ingredients

- 1/3 pound cooked salmon fillet
- 1/2 cup Greek yogurt
- 1/4 teaspoon salt
- 1 teaspoon dried dill weed
- 2 tablespoons butter, or to taste
- 4 slices French bread, or to taste
- 2 tablespoons prepared jalapeno pepper jelly, or to taste

Direction

- In a food processor, process dill weed, salt, Greek yogurt, and salmon until smooth and creamy. Chill for a minimum of 1 hour until the pate sets.
- Wipe butter on each bread slice and put in the toaster oven for 4 minutes to toast. Spread over the bread the salmon pate, and use pepper jelly to spread on top.

Nutrition Information

- Calories: 194 calories;
- Total Carbohydrate: 23.6 g
- Cholesterol: 22 mg
- Total Fat: 8.9 g
- Protein: 5.4 g
- Sodium: 393 mg

87. Gluten Free And Paleo Tuna Avocado Cups

""Excellently ripened avocado filled with a nutritious tuna salad that is packed with loads of flavor!""
Serving: 2 | Prep: 10m | Ready in: 10m

Ingredients

- 1 (5 ounce) can Bumble Bee® Solid White Albacore Tuna in Water, drained
- 2 tablespoons minced celery
- 2 tablespoons minced onion
- 2 tablespoons minced fresh dill
- 2 tablespoons olive oil mayonnaise
- 1/4 teaspoon celery salt
- 1/4 teaspoon dry mustard
- 1/8 teaspoon lemon pepper
- Kosher salt and freshly ground black pepper, to taste
- 1 large ripe avocado, halved, pitted
- Lemon wedges, for serving (optional)

Direction

- In a small bowl, lightly mix black pepper, lemon pepper, mustard, salt, mayo, dill, onion, celery and tuna together until just mixed.
- Fill the avocado halves with even amounts of the tuna. Serve right away with lemon wedges.

Nutrition Information

- Calories: 375 calories;

- Total Carbohydrate: 15.1 g
- Cholesterol: 37 mg
- Total Fat: 27.1 g
- Protein: 19.9 g
- Sodium: 731 mg

88. Golden Gazpacho Dip

"This soup is inspired by a dip. It calls for the brightest yellow squash and the most yellow tomatoes. While the dip sits, it can release liquid and you can strain it if you want."
Serving: 10 | Prep: 20m | Ready in: 20m

Ingredients

- 3/4 pound yellow tomatoes
- 1 yellow bell pepper, quartered, seeded, cut into large pieces
- 1 yellow squash, halved lengthwise and cut into large pieces
- 1 tablespoon cider vinegar or white balsamic vinegar
- 4 teaspoons olive oil
- 3/4 teaspoon salt
- 1/3 cup snipped fresh dill

Direction

- Remove the core of the tomatoes and use a knife to slice a shallow X under each tomato. Add cold water and ice to a bowl until filled. Put the tomatoes in a big pot of boiling water for 10 seconds to blanch. Take the tomatoes out using a slotted spoon and immediately put in the ice water. Peel the tomatoes, and then cut crosswise into two. Remove the seeds by squeezing the tomatoes over a bowl.
- In a food processor, pulse salt, olive oil, vinegar, squash, and pepper twice or thrice until very coarse. Slice the tomatoes into large pieces, add to the food processor together with dill, and pulse for a few times until blended but still a little lumpy. Enjoy immediately or refrigerate until ready to enjoy.

Nutrition Information

- Calories: 30 calories;
- Total Carbohydrate: 2.6 g
- Cholesterol: 0 mg
- Total Fat: 2.1 g
- Protein: 0.7 g
- Sodium: 184 mg

89. Greek Yogurt-and-dill-marinated Chicken

"This recipe is the one to make when you want a dish with chicken and yogurt."
Serving: 4 | Prep: 10m | Ready in: 3h25m

Ingredients

- 2 cups Greek yogurt
- 3 tablespoons extra-virgin olive oil
- 2 tablespoons sherry vinegar
- 4 teaspoons curry powder
- 1 teaspoon ground cumin
- 1/4 cup chopped fresh dill
- 2 cloves garlic, minced
- 1 tablespoon lemon zest
- ground black pepper to taste
- 4 (6 ounce) skinless, boneless chicken breast halves

Direction

- In a big bowl, mix together yogurt with cumin, curry powder, vinegar, and olive oil. Add lemon zest, garlic, and dill to the marinade. Use pepper to season.
- Dip the chicken in the marinade and coat thoroughly. Put a cover on the bowl and chill for 2-4 hours.
- Take the chicken out of the marinade, let sit for 30 minutes until the chicken meets room temperature.
- Start preheating the oven to 375°F (190°C). Use oil to lightly grease a baking pan.
- On the oil-coated pan, put the chicken; make sure to keep the chicken pieces apart.

- Put in the preheated oven and bake for 15 minutes. Turn and keep cooking for 25-30 minutes until the juices run clear and the chicken's middle is not pink anymore. When you insert an instant-read thermometer in the middle, it should display a minimum of 165°F (74°C).
- Take the chicken out of the oven and use aluminum foil to cover loosely. Let sit for 5 minutes and then enjoy.

Nutrition Information

- Calories: 408 calories;
- Total Carbohydrate: 6.5 g
- Cholesterol: 110 mg
- Total Fat: 24 g
- Protein: 39.6 g
- Sodium: 141 mg

90. Green Borscht

"This is a tasty and simple Russian soup with spinach and potatoes. The leftovers store in the fridge for 1 or 2 days. You can serve together with a dollop of sour cream."
Serving: 8 | Prep: 20m | Ready in: 50m

Ingredients

- 3 eggs, or more to taste
- 3 potatoes, cut into cubes, or more to taste
- 1/2 cup rice
- 1 bunch green onions, finely chopped
- salt to taste
- 1 bunch fresh spinach, stems removed and leaves chopped
- 1 bunch fresh parsley, chopped
- 1/4 cup sour cream, or more to taste
- 1 teaspoon chopped fresh dill, or more to taste

Direction

- Put the eggs in a saucepan and then add salted cold water to cover. Heat to boil, take out from the heat source, then cover the saucepan and allow the eggs to sit in the hot water for about 10 to 12 minutes. Drain off water from the saucepan and then add ice water to cover the eggs for about 10 minutes until refrigerate. Remove shell from eggs and then shred or chop.
- Add water in a large pot until halfway full and then heat to boil. Add green onions, rice and potatoes. Decrease the heat and let to simmer for 15 to 20 minutes until the potatoes are mostly tender. Add parsley and spinach and continue to simmer for 5 to 7 minutes until wilted.
- Mix sour cream into the soup until combined well. Place in dill. Heat the soup to boil again, then remove the pot from the heat source and mix the eggs into soup. Add salt to season.

Nutrition Information

- Calories: 167 calories;
- Total Carbohydrate: 27.7 g
- Cholesterol: 73 mg
- Total Fat: 3.8 g
- Protein: 7 g
- Sodium: 78 mg

91. Grilled Salmon Sandwich With Dill Sauce

"I prepared this sandwich once and have since become my favorite! It is a quick and simple dinner once you master its preparation. It tastes great either hot or cold."
Serving: 2 | Prep: 10m | Ready in: 25m

Ingredients

- 4 slices bacon
- 1 (1 pound) fillet salmon, cut into 2 portions
- 1 tablespoon olive oil
- 1/3 cup mayonnaise
- 1 teaspoon dried dill weed
- 1 teaspoon freshly grated lemon zest
- 4 slices country-style bread, toasted
- 4 slices tomato
- 2 green leaf lettuce leaves

Direction

- Over medium-high heat, cook bacon in a large, deep skillet for about 10 minutes until browned evenly. Drain the slices of bacon on a plate lined with paper towel.
- Preheat the outdoor grill over medium-high heat and oil the grate lightly. Use olive oil to evenly coat the salmon.
- Cook salmon on the grill, skin side down, for five minutes before turning and cooking the other side for 5 more minutes until skin can easily be lifted off the flesh. Turn the salmon one more time and continue to cook for about 2 to 3 minutes until salmon easily flakes with a fork.
- In a small bowl, whisk the lemon zest along with mayonnaise, and dill. Separate in two of the toasted bread slices. Top each with 1 lettuce leaf, 1 portion of cooked salmon, 2 bacon slices, 2 tomato slices and the remaining slice of toasted bread.

Nutrition Information

- Calories: 931 calories;
- Total Carbohydrate: 29.6 g
- Cholesterol: 145 mg
- Total Fat: 67 g
- Protein: 50.7 g
- Sodium: 1079 mg

92. Grilled Salmon Sandwich With Green Apple Slaw

"Experiment with this gourmet sandwich for a fresh alternative to usual sausages and burgers. It has a crunchy, sweet-tart apple and savory-glazed salmon topping."
Serving: 4 | Prep: 15m | Ready in: 25m

Ingredients

- 1/3 cup Heinz 57 Sauce, Lightly Flavoured
- 2 tablespoons melted butter
- 1 teaspoon Heinz Worcestershire Sauce
- 1 clove garlic, minced
- 4 skinless, boneless salmon fillets
- 1 Granny Smith apple, thinly sliced
- 1/2 cup very thinly sliced red onion
- 2 teaspoons lemon juice
- 2 teaspoons extra-virgin olive oil
- 2 teaspoons chopped fresh dill
- 1/4 teaspoon salt
- 1/4 teaspoon pepper
- 4 kaiser rolls
- Lettuce leaves

Direction

- Preheat a grill on medium-high heat. Line perforated non-stick foil onto the grate. Mix 57 sauce with garlic, butter, and Worcestershire sauce. Baste 1/2 of this mixture on salmon.
- Grill salmon for 4 to 5 minutes on each side while basting with the remaining sauce. Combine dill, onion and apples with pepper, salt, lemon juice, and oil. Cut the rolls in half and then lightly toast on the grill.
- Onto each halved roll, put a leaf of lettuce and then add a slice of salmon and same amounts of slaw.

Nutrition Information

- Calories: 378 calories;
- Total Carbohydrate: 34.1 g
- Cholesterol: 101 mg
- Total Fat: 14.4 g
- Protein: 27.9 g
- Sodium: 729 mg

93. Hearty Cabbage-rutabaga Slow Cooker Soup

"Use reduced or broth with no sodium for lower sodium content. This serves 6 people."
Serving: 6 | Prep: 25m | Ready in: 5h25m

Ingredients

- 1/4 large head cabbage, chopped
- 1/4 large rutabaga, diced

- 1 1/2 cups uncooked orzo pasta
- 1/2 large onion, finely chopped
- 1 whole head garlic, peeled and minced
- 3 tablespoons chopped fresh dill
- 6 cups water
- 2 cups vegetable broth

Direction

- In a slow cooker, put vegetable broth, water, dill, garlic, orzo pasta, onion, rutabaga and cabbage.
- Cover cooker. Cook for 5-9 hours on low until soup is thick and veggies are tender.

Nutrition Information

- Calories: 236 calories;
- Total Carbohydrate: 48.9 g
- Cholesterol: < mg
- Total Fat: 1.1 g
- Protein: 9 g
- Sodium: 182 mg

94. Herbed Feta Dip

"Pita chips, crackers, and veggies will taste better when enjoyed with this dip. It's tasty and has a low-fat content. You can refrigerate the dip overnight so that the flavors can develop."
Serving: 8 | Prep: 20m | Ready in: 20m

Ingredients

- 3/4 cup nonfat plain yogurt
- 1/2 cup crumbled feta cheese
- 1 (15 ounce) can cannellini beans, drained and rinsed
- 2 cloves garlic
- 1 tablespoon lemon juice
- 2 tablespoons chopped fresh parsley
- 2 tablespoons chopped fresh dill
- 2 tablespoons chopped fresh chives
- 2 tablespoons chopped fresh mint
- 1 teaspoon ground black pepper

Direction

- In the bowl of a food processor, put lemon juice, garlic, beans, feta, and yogurt and process until smooth. Add pepper, mint, chives, dill, and parsley; pulse until they are thoroughly blended. Move the dip to a serving bowl and refrigerate until ready to enjoy.

Nutrition Information

- Calories: 81 calories;
- Total Carbohydrate: 10.2 g
- Cholesterol: 9 mg
- Total Fat: 2.3 g
- Protein: 4.8 g
- Sodium: 233 mg

95. Herbed Zucchini Soup

"There are very few soups that are great for summer, and this one is one of them. You can refrigerate the soup to cool down a hot summer day."
Serving: 4 | Ready in: 20m

Ingredients

- 3 cups reduced-sodium chicken broth
- 1½ pounds zucchini, (about 3 medium), cut into 1-inch pieces
- 1 tablespoon chopped fresh tarragon, or dill or 1 teaspoon dried
- ¾ cup shredded reduced-fat Cheddar cheese, (3 ounces)
- ¼ teaspoon salt
- ¼ teaspoon freshly ground pepper

Direction

- In a medium-sized saucepan, put tarragon (or dill), zucchini, and broth. Boil over high heat. Lower to a simmer and cook without a cover for 7-10 minutes until the zucchini is soft. Put in a blender to puree until smooth (see tip), working in batches if needed. Transfer the soup back to the pan and heat over medium-high, gradually mixing in cheese until it is blended. Take away from heat and use pepper and salt to season. Enjoy cold or hot.

Nutrition Information

- Calories: 110 calories;
- Total Carbohydrate: 7 g
- Cholesterol: 15 mg
- Total Fat: 5 g
- Fiber: 2 g
- Protein: 10 g
- Sodium: 757 mg
- Sugar: 4 g
- Saturated Fat: 3 g

96. High Seas Chicken Souvlaki

"Serve this delicious grilled chicken with pita bread, vegetables, yogurt sauce and some slices of feta cheese.""
Serving: 4 | Prep: 20m | Ready in: 1h40m

Ingredients

- 8 bamboo skewers
- 1 cucumber - peeled, seeded, and shredded
- 1 (12 ounce) container Greek-style yogurt
- 2 cloves garlic, minced
- 2 sprigs fresh dill, chopped
- salt and freshly ground black pepper to taste
- 2 skinless, boneless chicken breasts, cut into 1/2-inch strips
- 2 sprigs fresh oregano, chopped
- 2 cloves garlic, minced
- 1 lemon, juiced
- 2 tablespoons extra-virgin olive oil
- salt and freshly ground black pepper to taste
- 3 Roma tomatoes, diced
- 1 cucumber - peeled, seeded, and diced
- 1/2 red onion, cut into thin 1-inch-long strips
- 2 tablespoons extra-virgin olive oil
- 1/2 lemon, juiced
- 8 pita bread rounds
- 4 ounces feta cheese, cut into 1/4-inch slices

Direction

- Steep bamboo skewers for 30-40 minutes in water.
- Place shredded cucumber in a fine mesh strainer and press to remove excess liquid; let drain for 15 minutes.
- In a small mixing bowl, combine pepper, salt, dill, shredded cucumber, 2 cloves minced garlic, and yogurt. Chill in the fridge.
- Place chicken in a bowl and add pepper salt, 2 tablespoons olive oil, lemon juice, 2 cloves minced garlic, and oregano; stir well to combine and chill for 20 minutes in the fridge.
- Set an outdoor grill to medium-high heat and grease the grate lightly with oil.
- In a mixing bowl, combine pepper, salt, 2 tablespoons olive oil, onion, diced cucumber, and tomatoes. Stir until well combined.
- Skewer the marinated chilled chicken.
- Grill the chicken, about 5 minutes per side until no longer pink inside and browned outside, add juice squeezed from 1/2 a lemon while cooking.
- Heat pita bread, 1 to 2 minutes per side on the grill until heated through. Top each pita bread round with tomato salad, 1 to 2 spoonfuls of yogurt sauce, and chicken from a skewer. Add feta cheese slices on top and serve.

Nutrition Information

- Calories: 688 calories;
- Total Carbohydrate: 70.1 g
- Cholesterol: 77 mg
- Total Fat: 31 g
- Protein: 31.9 g
- Sodium: 944 mg

97. Hot Off The Grill Potatoes

"Great potato slices!"
Serving: 5

Ingredients

- 3 tablespoons Melt® Organic Buttery Spread
- 5 medium potatoes, scrubbed and thinly sliced
- 1/4 cup chopped green onions
- 2 tablespoons chopped fresh parsley
- 2 tablespoons chopped fresh dill
- 2 tablespoons chopped fresh chives
- 2 tablespoons grated Parmesan cheese
- 1/4 teaspoon salt
- 1/4 teaspoon paprika
- 1/4 teaspoon black pepper
- 3 slices bacon, cooked and crumbled (optional)

Direction

- Fold 48x18-in. heavy foil piece in half to create 24x18-in. rectangle. Grease foil using 1 tbsp. melt organic buttery spread.
- In middle of foil, put potatoes. Sprinkle all spices, cheese and herbs. Put bacon on top (optional). Dot with leftover 2 tbsp. melt. Bring 2 opposite foil edges up; seal with double fold then fold leftover ends to enclose potatoes completely. Leave room for steam.
- Gas grill: Preheat grill. Lower heat to medium. On grill rack, put foil packet on heat. Cover. Grill till potatoes are tender, flipping packet each 10 minutes for about 30-40 minutes. Charcoal grill: put packet on medium coal s for same length of time.

Nutrition Information

- Calories: 218 calories;
- Total Carbohydrate: 30.7 g
- Cholesterol: 8 mg
- Total Fat: 8.4 g
- Protein: 5.7 g
- Sodium: 332 mg

98. Hudson's Baked Tilapia With Dill Sauce

"This tilapia is baked and seasoned with citrus and Cajun. You can enjoy it with lemon and dill sauce."
Serving: 4 | Prep: 10m | Ready in: 30m

Ingredients

- 4 (4 ounce) fillets tilapia
- salt and pepper to taste
- 1 tablespoon Cajun seasoning, or to taste
- 1 lemon, thinly sliced
- 1/4 cup mayonnaise
- 1/2 cup sour cream
- 1/8 teaspoon garlic powder
- 1 teaspoon fresh lemon juice
- 2 tablespoons chopped fresh dill

Direction

- Start preheating the oven to 350°F (175°C). Lightly oil a 9x13" baking plate.
- Use Cajun, pepper, and salt to season both sides of tilapia fillets. In the baking plate, put 1 layer of the seasoned fillets. Put on the fish fillets 1 layer of lemon slices. I often use 2 slices for each fillet to mostly cover the fish's surface.
- Put in the preheated oven and bake without a cover until a fork can easily flake the fish, about 15-20 minutes.
- As the fish bakes, in a small bowl, combine dill, lemon juice, garlic powder, sour cream, and mayonnaise. Enjoy with tilapia.

Nutrition Information

- Calories: 284 calories;
- Total Carbohydrate: 5.7 g
- Cholesterol: 59 mg
- Total Fat: 18.6 g
- Protein: 24.5 g
- Sodium: 501 mg

99. Hungarian Cucumber Salad

"Serve this refreshing cucumber salad during parties and backyard barbecues."
Serving: 6 | Prep: 15m | Ready in: 15m

Ingredients

- 2 large seedless English cucumbers, sliced thin
- 1 extra large onions, sliced thin
- 1/4 cup chopped fresh dill
- 3 tablespoons white vinegar
- 3 tablespoons vegetable oil
- 1 teaspoon salt, or to taste
- 1/2 teaspoon ground black pepper, or to taste

Direction

- In a big bowl, lightly stir together chopped dill, onion slices, and cucumber slices.
- Add vinegar over the mixture; mix well to coat.
- Add oil over the mixture; mix well to coat.
- Sprinkle black pepper and salt to season.

Nutrition Information

- Calories: 98 calories;
- Total Carbohydrate: 8.9 g
- Cholesterol: 0 mg
- Total Fat: 7 g
- Protein: 1.3 g
- Sodium: 393 mg

100. Jagic (Assyrian Cheese Spread)

"This cheese spread goes really well with a soft flat bread. Dill and herbs give it refreshing flavor.""
Serving: 20 | Prep: 25m | Ready in: 25m

Ingredients

- 1 cup butter, room temperature
- 1 (24 ounce) carton cottage cheese
- 3 green onions, minced
- 3 stalks celery, minced
- 1 jalapeno pepper, seeded and minced, or to taste
- 1 tablespoon chopped fresh dill
- 1/4 cup chopped fresh cilantro
- salt to taste

Direction

- Beat cottage cheese and butter together in a mixing bowl using a fork or whisk until no lumps remain. Mix in cilantro, dill, jalapeno, celery, and green onions. Add salt to taste.

Nutrition Information

- Calories: 119 calories;
- Total Carbohydrate: 1.3 g
- Cholesterol: 30 mg
- Total Fat: 10.8 g
- Protein: 4.5 g
- Sodium: 209 mg

101. Jalapeño & Dill Labneh

"A delicious labneh dip recipe added with herbs and a bit of hot pepper for a flavorful kick."
Serving: 8 | Prep: 20m | Ready in: 12h

Ingredients

- 1 quart (4 cups) low-fat plain yogurt
- ¼ teaspoon salt
- ¼ cup sliced scallions
- 1 small jalapeño pepper, sliced
- 1 tablespoon extra-virgin olive oil
- 1 tablespoon chopped fresh dill
- 1 tablespoon chopped fresh parsley
- ½ teaspoon toasted cumin seeds

Direction

- In a 7-inch or big fine-mesh sieve, line 4 layers of cheesecloth. Place it on top of the bowl, deep enough to leave at least 3 inches between the bowl and the bottom of the sieve. In a medium bowl, beat salt and yogurt then spoon it into the cheesecloth.

- Let it chill in the fridge for 12-24 hours until a cup of the liquid has drained in the bowl and the yogurt is slightly thick. Get rid of the liquid.
- Put cumin seeds, parsley, dill, oil, jalapeño and scallions on top then serve.

Nutrition Information

- Calories: 87 calories;
- Total Carbohydrate: 7 g
- Cholesterol: 7 mg
- Total Fat: 4 g
- Fiber: 0 g
- Protein: 6 g
- Sodium: 145 mg
- Sugar: 7 g
- Saturated Fat: 1 g

102. Kohlrabi And Pea Soup With Dill

"This vegetable soup smells so good and is great for summer days. I use my homegrown kohlrabi and peas to make this dish. Enjoy at room temperature."
Serving: 2 | Prep: 15m | Ready in: 45m

Ingredients

- 1 tablespoon olive oil
- 1/2 large onion, chopped
- 1 pound peas
- 1/2 pound kohlrabi, peeled and cut into small dice
- 1 bunch fresh dill, chopped
- 1/2 tablespoon seasoning blend (such as Vegeta®)
- water to cover

Direction

- In a saucepan, heat oil over medium heat. Add onion and cook for 3 minutes until wilted. Add kohlrabi and peas, toss to blend. Add seasoning blend and dill, toss to blend.
- Pour water to cover the vegetables and boil. Lower the heat and use a lid to cover halfway. Cook for another 20 minutes until the kohlrabi and peas are tender. Let cool to room temperature. Enjoy.

Nutrition Information

- Calories: 290 calories;
- Total Carbohydrate: 43.5 g
- Cholesterol: 0 mg
- Total Fat: 8 g
- Protein: 14.8 g
- Sodium: 983 mg

103. Kosher Chicken Soup With Matzo Balls

""You can cook this chicken soup in 45 minutes using a pressure cooker. If you simmer it for a longer period, you'll taste its amazing flavor and the herbs that fill matzo balls.""
Serving: 8 | Prep: 40m | Ready in: 14h

Ingredients

- For the Chicken Soup:
- 1 (2 1/2 to 3 pound) whole chicken, cut up
- 2 small yellow onions, diced
- 2 stalks celery, cut into chunks
- 3 carrots, cut into chunks
- 1 bunch fresh dill
- 1 bay leaf
- 3 quarts water
- For the Matzo Balls:
- 1/3 cup vegetable oil
- 4 eggs
- 2 tablespoons chopped fresh basil
- 1 tablespoon chopped fresh parsley
- 1 1/2 teaspoons salt
- 1/4 teaspoon ground black pepper
- 1 cup matzo meal
- 3 quarts water, or as needed
- 1 teaspoon salt

Direction

- To create the soup on stove top mix celery, bay leaf, 3 quarts of water, carrots, onions, dill, and chicken together in a big pot. Let the water boil before decreasing heat. Simmer it for 5 or more hours while partly covered. Stir the soup occasionally to take out any developing foam.
- Take vegetables and chicken from the broth. Throw out veggies. Drain the broth and let it cool in the fridge overnight. When chicken can be handled, remove its meat from bones. Shred the meat into pieces, put a cover on and refrigerate chicken.
- For the pressure cooker users, combine onions, bay leaf, water, celery, dill, carrots, onions, and chicken in pressure cooker. Seal it tightly and build it up to full pressure. Decrease heat, keeping pressure full, 30 minutes. Let the pressure naturally release. Take the vegetables and chicken from the broth. Drain the broth and discard the vegetables. When chicken can be handled take the meat off bones.
- In a mixing bowl, blend well parsley, black pepper, basil, vegetable oil, 1 1/2 tsp. of salt, and eggs. Add the matzo meal and seal the bowl with some plastic wrap. Store it in the refrigerator for 60 minutes.
- Boil 1 tsp. salt and 3 or more quarts of water in a big pot. Wet your hands and carefully form matzo mixture in 2-in. balls. Drop balls into boiling water and simmer 20 minutes.
- Get rid of the fat on the cold chicken broth and transfer broth to a pot. Heat the pot on medium heat, and then add salt to taste and saved cooked chicken, if you want. Add the cooked matzo balls into the chicken soup. Serve hot.

Nutrition Information

- Calories: 511 calories;
- Total Carbohydrate: 18.2 g
- Cholesterol: 148 mg
- Total Fat: 40.7 g
- Protein: 18.6 g
- Sodium: 860 mg

104. Kosher Seasoning Salt

"I make a homemade seasoning salt to accompany kosher salt. It tastes just as delicious as the one you buy at the store."

Serving: 48 | Prep: 5m | Ready in: 5m

Ingredients

- 7 tablespoons kosher salt
- 2 teaspoons paprika
- 1 teaspoon dried thyme leaves
- 1 teaspoon dried parsley
- 1 teaspoon dry mustard powder
- 1 teaspoon garlic powder
- 1/2 teaspoon chili powder
- 1/4 teaspoon curry powder
- 1/4 teaspoon ground cumin
- 1/4 teaspoon dried dill weed

Direction

- In a small mixing bowl, put the salt. Mix in dill, cumin, curry powder, chili powder, garlic powder, mustard powder, parsley, thyme, and paprika until evenly combined. Preserve in a shaker jar with a tight seal.

Nutrition Information

- Calories: 1 calorie;
- Total Carbohydrate: 0.2 g
- Cholesterol: 0 mg
- Total Fat: 0 g
- Protein: 0.1 g
- Sodium: 840 mg

105. Labneh (Lebanese Yogurt)

"This amazing dish makes a really great spread for breads and dip for vegetables! You may also place it on top of almost any dish!"
Serving: 12 | Prep: 10m | Ready in: 10m

Ingredients

- 1 1/2 cups Greek yogurt
- 1/4 cup extra-virgin olive oil
- 1 tablespoon chopped fresh mint
- 1 tablespoon chopped fresh dill
- 1/2 teaspoon kosher salt, or to taste

Direction

- In a bowl, combine the dill, kosher salt, mint, Greek yogurt and olive oil together. Cover the mixture and keep it in the fridge for up to 12 hours.

Nutrition Information

- Calories: 75 calories;
- Total Carbohydrate: 1 g
- Cholesterol: 6 mg
- Total Fat: 7.2 g
- Protein: 1.5 g
- Sodium: 96 mg

106. Lamb And Potato Skillet

"This recipe belongs to my Grandmother. You can serve this dish with spinach to complete a meal. Two green onions can be used instead of leek."
Serving: 4 | Prep: 25m | Ready in: 1h

Ingredients

- 1 tablespoon vegetable oil
- 1 leek, chopped
- 1 cup chopped fresh mushrooms
- 1 pound ground lamb
- 1 clove garlic, minced
- 3/4 cup beef broth
- 1 tablespoon chopped fresh dill
- 1/2 teaspoon garlic and herb seasoning blend
- 1/4 teaspoon ground black pepper
- 1/4 teaspoon onion powder
- 1 bay leaf
- 3 cups chopped potatoes
- 1 (6.5 ounce) can tomato sauce
- 1/2 head cabbage, cored and shredded

Direction

- In a frying pan, heat oil over medium heat. Mix in mushrooms and leeks for 8 minutes until they start to get tender. Add lamb to the frying pan and break into small pieces; add garlic and cook, tossing sometimes, for 8 minutes until the lamb is not pink anymore. Strain the liquid from the pan.
- Mix in potatoes, bay leaf, onion powder, pepper, herb seasoning blend, garlic, dill, and broth. Boil it, then lower the heat to low. Put a cover on and simmer for 12 minutes until the potatoes are nearly soft. Add shredded cabbage and tomato sauce. Raise the heat to medium and simmer with a cover for 5-7 minutes until the potatoes are soft and the cabbage is cooked.
- Take out the bay leaf and enjoy.

Nutrition Information

- Calories: 412 calories;
- Total Carbohydrate: 35.6 g
- Cholesterol: 76 mg
- Total Fat: 19.4 g
- Protein: 25.7 g
- Sodium: 493 mg

107. Lemon & Dill Chicken

"This pan sauce is inspired by Greek food. It has dill and lemon and is perfect to enjoy with sautéed chicken breasts. Pair it with whole-wheat orzo and roasted broccoli and you will have a full meal."
Serving: 4 | Ready in: 30m

Ingredients

- 4 boneless, skinless chicken breasts, (1-1¼ pounds)
- Salt & freshly ground pepper, to taste
- 3 teaspoons extra-virgin olive oil, or canola oil, divided
- ¼ cup finely chopped onion
- 3 cloves garlic, minced
- 1 cup reduced-sodium chicken broth
- 2 teaspoons flour
- 2 tablespoons chopped fresh dill, divided
- 1 tablespoon lemon juice

Direction

- Use pepper and salt to season both sides of the chicken breasts. In a big heavy frying pan, heat 1 1/2 teaspoons of oil over medium-high heat. Add chicken and sear for 3 minutes each side until both sides are browned well. Move the chicken to a dish and use foil to make a tent.
- Lower the heat to medium. Add to the pan the rest of 1 1/2 teaspoons of oil. Add garlic and onion, stir and cook for 1 minute. In a measuring cup, combine lemon juice, 1 tablespoon of dill, flour, and broth and add to the pan. Cook, stirring, for 3 minutes until thickened slightly.
- Put any accumulated juices and the chicken back to the pan, lower the heat to low and simmer for 4 minutes until the chicken is thoroughly cooked. Move the chicken to a warm dish. Use pepper and salt to season the sauce and ladle over the chicken. Use the rest of 1 tablespoon chopped fresh dill to garnish.

Nutrition Information

- Calories: 170 calories;
- Total Carbohydrate: 3 g
- Cholesterol: 63 mg
- Total Fat: 6 g
- Fiber: 0 g
- Protein: 24 g
- Sodium: 339 mg
- Sugar: 1 g
- Saturated Fat: 1 g

108. Lemon Dill Salad Dressing

""The addition of lots of dill and zesty lemon juice made this dressing even more tasty!""
Serving: 12 | Prep: 10m | Ready in: 10m

Ingredients

- 2 cups mayonnaise
- 1/2 cup lemon juice
- 1/4 cup dried dill weed to taste
- 1/2 cup buttermilk

Direction

- Mix the buttermilk, dill, lemon juice and mayonnaise together in a medium-sized bowl. Keep in the fridge until it's time to serve.

Nutrition Information

- Calories: 272 calories;
- Total Carbohydrate: 3.1 g
- Cholesterol: 14 mg
- Total Fat: 29.2 g
- Protein: 0.9 g
- Sodium: 221 mg

109. Lemon Dill Salmon Fillet

"These salmon fillets are steamed perfectly in foil and it will be great to enjoy with homemade tartar sauce."
Serving: 4 | Prep: 25m | Ready in: 50m

Ingredients

- 1/2 pound baby red and yellow potatoes, or to taste
- 1 cup fresh green beans, trimmed, or to taste
- 2 tablespoons olive oil, divided
- 2 (6 ounce) salmon fillets
- 1 clove garlic, crushed
- 1 sprig chopped fresh dill
- 1/2 lemon, sliced
- 1/2 lemon, juiced
- 1/2 teaspoon freshly ground black pepper
- 1/3 teaspoon coarse salt
- Tartar Sauce:
- 3 tablespoons mayonnaise
- 1 1/2 tablespoons capers, roughly chopped
- 1 lemon, juiced
- 1/2 teaspoon freshly ground black pepper
- 1/4 teaspoon salt

Direction

- Start preheating the oven to 325°F (165°C).
- In a saucepan, insert a steamer and add water until just beneath the steamer's bottom. Boil the water. Add green beans and potatoes, put a cover on, and steam for 10 minutes until soft. Strain.
- Brush 1 teaspoon of olive oil on the shiny side of 2 big aluminum foil sheets. Put the salmon with the skin-side turning down in the middle. Use garlic and the rest of the olive oil to brush over the salmon. Drizzle over the top with dill. Distribute slices of lemon over the salmon; extract 1/2 lemon on top. Use 1/3 teaspoon salt and 1/2 teaspoon pepper to season.
- Use 2 sheets of aluminum foil to cover the salmon, shiny side turning down. Fold all sides of the aluminum foil inwards to make a pouch. Move pouches to a cookie sheet.
- Put in the preheated oven and bake for 10-12 minutes until a fork can easily flake the salmon.
- To prepare a tartar sauce, in a small bowl, combine capers and mayonnaise. Mix in 1/4 teaspoon salt, 1/2 teaspoon pepper, and juice from 1 lemon.
- Enjoy the salmon with tartar sauce and steamed green beans and potatoes.

Nutrition Information

- Calories: 283 calories;
- Total Carbohydrate: 14.4 g
- Cholesterol: 40 mg
- Total Fat: 18 g
- Protein: 17.5 g
- Sodium: 537 mg

110. Mama H's Fooled You Fancy Slow Cooker Turkey Breast

"I made this turkey breast dish with my home-made onion soup and some other ingredients. It is really flavorful.""
Serving: 6 | Prep: 20m | Ready in: 5h20m

Ingredients

- 1/2 bunch fresh flat-leaf parsley, divided
- 1/2 bunch dill, divided
- 1 clementine, peeled and segmented, divided
- 1 (2 1/2 to 3 pound) turkey breast
- 2 2/3 tablespoons dried onion flakes
- 1 1/2 teaspoons dried parsley
- 1 teaspoon ground turmeric
- 1 teaspoon onion powder
- 1/2 teaspoon salt, or to taste
- 1/2 teaspoon white sugar, or to taste
- 1/2 teaspoon celery seed
- 1/4 teaspoon ground black pepper
- 1 (16 ounce) can whole berry cranberry sauce

Direction

- Place into the bottom and slightly up the sides of a slow cooker with at least 1/2 fresh parsley

and 1/2 dill. Top with sprinkled 1/2 the clementine section. Add turkey breast.
- In a mixing bowl, combine black pepper, celery seed, sugar, salt, onion powder, turmeric, dried parsley, and onion flakes and stir well. Liberally sprinkle the spice mixture over the turkey breast in the slow cooker.
- Ladle dollops of cranberry sauce all over the turkey breast and in every corner of the pot of the slow cooker. Add remaining dill and fresh parsley, and finally the remaining clementine sections. Cook for about 5 hours on low power until the center of turkey breast is no longer pink and juices run clear, checking the turkey after 4.5 hours to make sure it's not overcooked.

Nutrition Information

- Calories: 417 calories;
- Total Carbohydrate: 32.4 g
- Cholesterol: 170 mg
- Total Fat: 6.3 g
- Protein: 55.6 g
- Sodium: 316 mg

111. Maple Dill Carrots

"My friends ask for this recipe all the time when it comes to dinner. This is a great combination among carrots, dill, brown sugar, and melted butter.""
Serving: 4 | Prep: 10m | Ready in: 20m

Ingredients

- 3 cups peeled and sliced carrots
- 2 tablespoons butter
- 2 tablespoons brown sugar
- 1 1/2 tablespoons chopped fresh dill
- 1/2 teaspoon salt
- 1/2 teaspoon black pepper

Direction

- Pour water into a skillet just enough to cover carrots. Bring to a boil over medium heat. Simmer until carrots are softened and liquid has vaporized. Mix in pepper, salt, dill, brown sugar, and butter

Nutrition Information

- Calories: 117 calories;
- Total Carbohydrate: 16.1 g
- Cholesterol: 15 mg
- Total Fat: 6 g
- Protein: 1 g
- Sodium: 401 mg

112. Mast-o-khiar

"A dip that means yogurt and cucumber. It's a crowd pleaser and hence, common at Persian parties. Some recipes have herbs while others have added garlic. You can add both if desired. Stud with raisins and walnuts."
Serving: 6 | Prep: 10m | Ready in: 10m

Ingredients

- 2 cups plain yogurt
- 1/4 cup sour cream
- 1 teaspoon dried dill
- 1 teaspoon dried mint
- 1/2 cup raisins
- 1/2 cucumber, peeled and diced
- 1/2 cup chopped walnuts

Direction

- In a bowl, combine together mint, dill, yogurt, and sour cream. Mix in walnuts, cucumber, and raisins. Pour the mixture into a serving dish.

Nutrition Information

- Calories: 126 calories;
- Total Carbohydrate: 12.8 g
- Cholesterol: 4 mg
- Total Fat: 8.4 g
- Protein: 2.3 g
- Sodium: 7 mg

113. Meze Fava Beans

"Fava beans are a traditional Turkish meal, prepared with onions and served with garlic yogurt at room temperature."
Serving: 12 | Prep: 15m | Ready in: 30m

Ingredients

- 3 tablespoons olive oil
- 1/2 onion, chopped
- 1 1/2 pounds fresh fava beans, shelled
- 2 tablespoons water
- 1 teaspoon all-purpose flour
- 1 cup boiling water
- 1 teaspoon lemon juice
- 1/2 teaspoon white sugar
- salt to taste
- 1/2 cup chopped fresh dill

Direction

- Add oil to a pan and heat it up on medium heat. Add in onions; stir onions frying them for about 1 minute until fragrant. Add in fava beans and sauté for 2 minutes, making it soft.
- In separate bowl combine flour and 2 tablespoons of water and mix it well; add the mixture into the pan with fava bean. Add lemon juice, sugar, salt, and a cup of water. Place the pan cover and bring the mixture to the boil. Reduce the heat to low and simmer about 5 minutes until fava beans are very soft.
- Add dill into the softened fava beans; simmer for 2 additional minutes until all flavors are well combined. Let the dish cool to room temperature.

Nutrition Information

- Calories: 229 calories;
- Total Carbohydrate: 34.4 g
- Cholesterol: 0 mg
- Total Fat: 4.3 g
- Protein: 15 g
- Sodium: 22 mg

114. Mizeria (polish Cucumber Salad)

"Polish style cucumber salad"
Serving: 12 | Prep: 10m | Ready in: 45m

Ingredients

- 1 pound small cucumbers, peeled and thinly sliced
- salt to taste
- 1 bunch dill, chopped
- 2 1/2 tablespoons sour cream
- 1 teaspoon lemon juice
- 1 pinch white sugar
- ground black pepper to taste

Direction

- In a bowl, sprinkle salt on top of cucumbers. Let it sit for about 5 minutes until the cucumbers become soft. Squeeze out liquid from the cucumbers and get rid of it. Put dill into the cucumbers.
- In a bowl, mix sugar, lemon juice and sour cream. Stir in the cucumbers then toss until coated. Sprinkle black pepper to season. Let it totally chill for a minimum of 30 minutes prior to serving.

Nutrition Information

- Calories: 13 calories;
- Total Carbohydrate: 1.4 g
- Cholesterol: 1 mg
- Total Fat: 0.7 g
- Protein: 0.4 g
- Sodium: 4 mg

115. Mloda Kapusta Z Koperkiem (Spring Cabbage With Dill)

"A great side dish made with spring cabbage."
Serving: 4 | Prep: 15m | Ready in: 45m

Ingredients

- 1 head cabbage, cored and shredded
- 1 bunch fresh dill, chopped
- 2 tablespoons unsalted butter
- 2 teaspoons vegetable stock powder
- 2/3 cup water, or more to taste
- 1/4 cup sour cream
- salt and ground black pepper to taste

Direction

- In a pot, mix the vegetable stock powder, butter, dill and cabbage, pour in water to cover. Let it simmer on low heat for about 30 minutes, stirring once in a while, until the cabbage becomes soft. Take off from heat.
- In a small bowl, mix together the salt, sour cream and 2 tablespoons of cooking liquid. Stir it into the cabbage mixture until well incorporated. Put pepper and salt to season.

Nutrition Information

- Calories: 159 calories;
- Total Carbohydrate: 18.3 g
- Cholesterol: 22 mg
- Total Fat: 9.2 g
- Protein: 4.6 g
- Sodium: 109 mg

116. Mom's Dill Dip

"Chopped veggies will taste much better with this dip. It is great to be enjoyed as an appetizer or a part of a light meal."
Serving: 8 | Prep: 10m | Ready in: 10m

Ingredients

- 1 cup sour cream
- 1 cup mayonnaise
- 1 tablespoon dried parsley flakes
- 1 tablespoon finely chopped green onions (white portion only)
- 1 teaspoon dried dill weed
- 1 teaspoon seasoned salt (such as Spice Islands® Beau Monde Seasoning)

Direction

- In a bowl, whisk together seasoned salt, dill, green onion, parsley, mayonnaise, and sour cream until smooth.

Nutrition Information

- Calories: 260 calories;
- Total Carbohydrate: 2.3 g
- Cholesterol: 23 mg
- Total Fat: 27.9 g
- Protein: 1.2 g
- Sodium: 173 mg

117. Mushroom Melt With Dill Aioli

"If you're already tired of the ordinary grilled cheese, this recipe is the right one to make. The aioli will be a big hit. The aioli will harden in the fridge because of the olive oil, but it will soften quickly."
Serving: 1 | Prep: 15m | Ready in: 25m

Ingredients

- Aioli:
- 1 garlic clove, chopped
- 1 teaspoon lemon juice
- 1 egg yolk
- 1/4 cup olive oil
- 1 teaspoon dried dill weed
- 1/2 teaspoon salt
- cayenne pepper, to taste
- Sandwich:
- 2 tablespoons butter
- 2 slices whole wheat bread
- 4 thick slices Cheddar cheese
- 2 large mushrooms, chopped

- 1 cup fresh baby spinach

Direction

- In a bowl, mix together lemon juice and garlic, lightly stir egg yolk in. Add cayenne, salt, dill, and olive oil; toss the aioli until blended.
- Place a big frying pan on medium heat. Wipe butter on one side of each slice of bread; put on the frying pan with the buttered side turning down. Put on the bread the spinach, mushrooms, and 2 Cheddar cheese slices. Top with the 2 remaining Cheddar cheese slices and the remaining bread slice, buttered side turning up. Fry the sandwich for 5 minutes each side until crispy and dark brown. Enjoy with aioli dip.

Nutrition Information

- Calories: 1816 calories;
- Total Carbohydrate: 31.7 g
- Cholesterol: 504 mg
- Total Fat: 159 g
- Protein: 69.5 g
- Sodium: 3043 mg

118. Orzo Salad With Salmon, Herbs, And Yogurt Vinaigrette

"'orzo' is a rice-shaped pasta known that is great for salads. In this recipe, it is topped with a low-fat yogurt dressing which is also delectable on a green salad or grilled chicken."
Serving: 4 | Prep: 25m | Ready in: 41m

Ingredients

- 1 cup orzo pasta
- Vinaigrette:
- 1/3 cup plain low-fat yogurt
- 2 tablespoons fresh lemon juice
- 2 tablespoons extra-virgin olive oil
- 1 tablespoon honey
- 1 teaspoon lemon zest
- 1/4 teaspoon coarse salt
- 1/8 teaspoon freshly ground black pepper
- Salad:
- 1 cup halved cherry tomatoes
- 1 cup peeled and diced English cucumber
- 3 3/4 ounces canned salmon, drained and flaked
- 1 tablespoon minced fresh parsley
- 1 1/2 teaspoons minced fresh chives
- 1 1/2 teaspoons minced fresh dill

Direction

- Bring to boil lightly salted water in a large pot and add orzo in the boiling water. Cook while stirring often for about 11 minutes until tender but firm to bite. Drain off water and place in a large bowl.
- In a bowl, whisk lemon zest, yogurt, honey, pepper, salt, lemon juice, and olive oil together until the vinaigrette becomes smooth.
- Combine chives, salmon, dill, tomatoes, parsley, and cucumber with the orzo. Toss in vinaigrette until coated.

Nutrition Information

- Calories: 332 calories;
- Total Carbohydrate: 46.7 g
- Cholesterol: 13 mg
- Total Fat: 9.9 g
- Protein: 14.7 g
- Sodium: 264 mg

119. Oven-baked Cod With Bread Crumbs

"The easiest recipe of baked cod."
Serving: 4 | Prep: 10m | Ready in: 30m

Ingredients

- 4 (4 ounce) cod fillets
- 1 pinch salt and freshly ground black pepper to taste
- 1/2 cup warm water
- 1/2 fish bouillon cube
- 3/4 cup dry bread crumbs

- 1/4 cup butter, cut into small chunks
- 1 bunch fresh parsley, chopped
- 1 tablespoon chopped fresh dill
- 2 teaspoons dried tarragon

Direction

- Preheat the oven to 200 degrees C (400 degrees F). In a baking dish, lay the cod fillets and use pepper and salt to season a bit.
- In a bowl, mix fish bouillon cube and water. Mix to combine and add on top of cod.
- Using a fork to combine pepper, salt, tarragon, dill, parsley, butter and breadcrumbs in a bowl till crumbly. Drizzle equally on top of cod.
- Bake in the preheated oven for roughly 20 minutes till crust becomes crunchy and golden and the fish could be flaked easily using a fork.

Nutrition Information

- Calories: 283 calories;
- Total Carbohydrate: 16 g
- Cholesterol: 72 mg
- Total Fat: 13.5 g
- Protein: 23.8 g
- Sodium: 361 mg

120. Oven-baked Salmon With Herbs

"This is a flavor and super simple oven-baked salmon dish. Feel free to try out other fresh herbs or even a mixture of spring onion, dill, and parsley if you don't like dill."
Serving: 6 | Prep: 15m | Ready in: 1h

Ingredients

- 1 cup chopped fresh dill
- 3 tablespoons olive oil
- 1 lemon, juiced
- 1 tablespoon honey
- 2 cloves garlic, finely minced, or more to taste
- 1 teaspoon ground coriander
- salt and ground black pepper to taste
- 1 (2.5 pound) boneless salmon fillet

Direction

- In a small bowl, mix dill, garlic, pepper, salt, olive oil, honey, lemon juice, and coriander.
- Rinse the salmon fillet with cold running water and then pat dry using paper towels. Spread the salmon onto a large piece of plastic wrap with the skin-side down. Pour the dill mixture around the top of fish, then wrap properly with plastic wrap and chill for half an hour.
- Preheat an oven to 220 degrees C (425 degrees F). Remove wrap from salmon and transfer to a baking dish with the skin-side down.
- Bake in the oven for about 12 to 15 minutes until the fish easily flakes with a fork.

Nutrition Information

- Calories: 284 calories;
- Total Carbohydrate: 5.7 g
- Cholesterol: 81 mg
- Total Fat: 13.3 g
- Protein: 35.1 g
- Sodium: 116 mg

121. Oven-roasted Fish With Peas And Tomatoes

"You can serve this dish at a dinner party or a family meal."
Serving: 4 | Prep: 20m | Ready in: 40m

Ingredients

- 1¼ pounds skinless cod or ocean perch fillets
- 2 cups frozen peas, thawed
- 1 cup fresh button mushrooms, halved
- ¾ cup grape tomatoes
- 1 small onion, cut into very thin wedges
- 4 teaspoons olive oil, divided
- ¼ teaspoon salt, divided
- ¼ teaspoon ground black pepper, divided

- 2 teaspoons snipped fresh dill or ½ teaspoon dried dill

Direction

- Wash the fish, use paper towels to tap dry. Slice the fish into 4 pieces about serving-size if needed.
- Start preheating the oven to 425°F. Use cooking spray to lightly coat a big rimmed cookie sheet. Mix onion, tomatoes, mushrooms, and peas together in a medium-sized bowl. Use 3 teaspoons of oil to drizzle and 1/8 teaspoon each of pepper and salt to sprinkle; stir to coat. On 1 side of the prepared pan, put the vegetables. Roast in the oven for 10 minutes.
- In the pan beside the vegetable mixture, put the fish fillets with the thin portions turning down. Use the rest of the 1 teaspoon oil to brush and the rest of 1/8 teaspoon each pepper and salt to sprinkle. Mix the vegetable mixture. Roast until the vegetables are soft and a fork can easily flake the fish, about 12 minutes.
- For serving, move the vegetables and fish to 4 serving dishes. Use dill to sprinkle.

Nutrition Information

- Calories: 228 calories;
- Total Carbohydrate: 13 g
- Cholesterol: 60 mg
- Total Fat: 6 g
- Fiber: 4 g
- Protein: 30 g
- Sodium: 306 mg
- Sugar: 6 g
- Saturated Fat: 1 g

122. Pan-seared Salmon With Fennel & Dill Salsa

"This tomato-based salsa has an interesting crunchy texture from fennel that also goes really well with seared salmon. Serve this with whole-wheat couscous and a glass of rose wine."

Serving: 4 | Ready in: 30m

Ingredients

- 1 large tomato, chopped
- 1 cup finely chopped fennel (about ½ bulb, stalks trimmed)
- 2 tablespoons minced red onion
- 2 tablespoons minced dill
- 1 tablespoon red-wine vinegar
- ½ teaspoon salt, divided
- 1 pound salmon fillet, skinned (see Tip)
- 2 tablespoons extra-virgin olive oil
- Freshly ground pepper to taste

Direction

- In a medium mixing bowl, combine 1/4 teaspoon salt, vinegar, dill, onion, fennel, and tomato.
- Divide salmon into 4 equal portions, add pepper and remaining 1/4 teaspoon salt to season. In a large nonstick pan, heat oil over high heat until oil starts shimmering, not smoking. Add seasoned salmon, skinned-side up and cook for 3 to 5 minutes until golden brown. Flip salmon over and turn off the heat. Let the salmon cook without external heat for 3 to 5 more minutes until just cooked through. Serve right away with salsa.

Nutrition Information

- Calories: 316 calories;
- Total Carbohydrate: 4 g
- Cholesterol: 62 mg
- Total Fat: 22 g
- Fiber: 1 g
- Protein: 24 g
- Sodium: 372 mg
- Sugar: 2 g

- Saturated Fat: 4 g
- Sodium: 811 mg

123. Pasta With Creamy Smoked Salmon And Dill

"This amazing pasta dish is made with home-smoked salmon. You can make any pasta shape that you like."
Serving: 8 | Prep: 25m | Ready in: 40m

Ingredients

- 8 cups uncooked penne pasta
- sea salt to taste
- 2 1/2 cups chopped smoked salmon
- 1 cup cream cheese
- 1 cup chopped fresh dill
- 5 green onions, chopped
- 2 tablespoons Dijon mustard
- 1 teaspoon grated lemon zest
- 1 tablespoon fresh lemon juice
- ground black pepper to taste

Direction

- Add water to a big pot to fill. Add sea salt to taste, and boil until rolling. Mix in penne and boil again. Cook without a cover, tossing sometimes for 11 minutes, until the pasta is cooked thoroughly but not mushy.
- Strain the penne thoroughly, saving 1 cup of the pasta cooking water.
- Put the saved cup of pasta water and penne back to the empty pot and put on medium-low heat.
- Mix black pepper, lemon juice, lemon zest, Dijon mustard, green onions, dill, cream cheese, and smoked salmon into the pasta for 4-5 minutes until the cream cheese melts.

Nutrition Information

- Calories: 418 calories;
- Total Carbohydrate: 55.2 g
- Cholesterol: 42 mg
- Total Fat: 13.7 g
- Protein: 19.9 g

124. Poached Halibut With Herbed Vinaigrette

"Impart the flavor by letting mild fish simmer gently in a fragrant and simple broth. Don't overcook or overcrowd the fish to prevent falling apart."
Serving: 4 | Ready in: 50m

Ingredients

- Broth
- 8 cups water
- 1 cup red-wine vinegar
- 1 medium onion, halved
- 1 medium carrot, quartered
- 1 stalk celery, quartered
- 3 cloves garlic, unpeeled, halved
- 1 tablespoon salt
- 1 teaspoon peppercorns
- 1 bay leaf
- 1 sprig fresh thyme
- Halibut & Vinaigrette
- 4 6-ounce halibut steaks, 1 inch thick, skinned
- Salt & freshly ground pepper, to taste
- 2 tablespoons lemon juice
- 1 tablespoon Dijon mustard
- 2 teaspoons reduced-fat sour cream
- 2 tablespoons canola oil
- 1 medium shallot, finely chopped
- 1 tablespoon coarsely chopped fresh Italian parsley
- 1 tablespoon coarsely chopped fresh tarragon
- 1 tablespoon chopped fresh chives
- 2 teaspoons coarsely chopped fresh dill, plus sprigs for garnish

Direction

- For the broth: In a large pot, combine all of the broth ingredients. Boil then decrease to low heat and let simmer for 30 minutes, uncovered. In a large deep skillet, strain the broth and remove solids.

- For halibut poaching and vinaigrette: Simmer broth. Add pepper and salt on both sides of halibut to season. Place halibut into the broth and poach for 5-10 minutes till the center is opaque, uncovered.
- In the meantime, in a small bowl, add 2 tbsp. of simmering broth. Add sour cream, mustard and lemon juice. Add oil and whisk slowly. Place in shallot; add pepper and salt to taste. Take halibut out of the poaching liquid and distribute into 4 warmed plates. Stir chopped dill, chives, tarragon and parsley into the vinaigrette and place on top of the fish. Add dill sprigs for garnish. Serve straight away.

Nutrition Information

- Calories: 234 calories;
- Total Carbohydrate: 3 g
- Cholesterol: 84 mg
- Total Fat: 10 g
- Fiber: 0 g
- Protein: 32 g
- Sodium: 283 mg
- Sugar: 1 g
- Saturated Fat: 1 g

125. Polish Zucchini Salad

"A Polish zucchini salad with garlic, dill and yogurt."
Serving: 6 | Prep: 5m | Ready in: 5m

Ingredients

- 1/4 cup plain yogurt
- 2 tablespoons chopped fresh dill
- 1 clove garlic, minced
- salt
- 2 fresh zucchini, thinly sliced

Direction

- In a bowl, mix the garlic, dill and yogurt, then put salt to taste. Slowly stir in the sliced zucchini.

Nutrition Information

- Calories: 12 calories;
- Total Carbohydrate: 2.4 g
- Cholesterol: 0 mg
- Total Fat: 0.1 g
- Protein: 0.9 g
- Sodium: 33 mg

126. Pop's Dill Pickles

"I've been making this recipe for years. Recently, I've started to add garlic cloves and the result is amazing. The longer your pickle ferments, the better it tastes."
Serving: 35 | Prep: 30m | Ready in: 2h45m

Ingredients

- 8 pounds small pickling cucumbers
- 4 cups water
- 4 cups distilled white vinegar
- 3/4 cup white sugar
- 1/2 cup pickling salt
- 3 tablespoons pickling spice, wrapped in cheesecloth
- 7 1-quart canning jars with lids and rings
- 7 heads fresh dill
- 7 cloves garlic

Direction

- In a big pot, put cucumbers and fill it with ice cubes. Allow them to stand for a minimum of 2 hours, but no longer than 8 hours. Strain and tap dry.
- In a saucepan, put pickling spice, pickling salt, sugar, vinegar, and water. Boil, then simmer for 15 minutes.
- Put the lids and the jars in boiling water for a minimum of 5 minutes to sterilize. In the sterilized, hot jars, pack the cucumbers and fill the jars leaving 1/2-inch headspace. Put into each jar 1 clove of garlic and 1 dill head. Add the hot pickling liquid into the jars, filling to within 1/4 inch until reaching the rim. Use a moist paper towel to clean the rims of the jars

and remove any extra food. Screw the lids on top.
- In the bottom of a big stockpot, put a rack and add water until filled halfway. Boil over high heat, then use a holder to gently lower the jars into the pot. Keep a 2-inch space between the jars. Add more boiling water if needed until the water is above the jars by a minimum of 1 inch. Bring to a rolling boil, put a cover on the pot, and boil until the time your county Extension agent recommended, about 5 minutes.
- Take the jars out of the stockpot and put on a wood or a cloth-covered surface, keep them a few inches apart, until cool. When they're cool, press 1 finger on the top of each lid to make sure that the seal is tight. (The lid doesn't move down or up). If you find any loosely-sealed jars, chill them and eat within 2 weeks. Preserve in a dark, cool area, and wait for a minimum of 1 week before opening.

Nutrition Information

- Calories: 35 calories;
- Total Carbohydrate: 8.5 g
- Cholesterol: 0 mg
- Total Fat: 0.1 g
- Protein: 0.7 g
- Sodium: 1585 mg

127. Puff Pastry Chicken 'n Broccoli Pot Pie

"TA puff pastry pie stuffed with slivered almonds, dill, onion, red pepper, broccoli, and chicken, and a few more ingredients, all combine with mayo."
Serving: 12 | Prep: 35m | Ready in: 1h5m

Ingredients

- cooking spray
- 4 cups diced deli rotisserie chicken
- 1 1/2 cups shredded Mexican cheese blend
- 1 cup mayonnaise (such as Hellman's®)
- 1 cup finely chopped broccoli florets
- 1/2 cup diced onion
- 1/3 cup finely chopped red bell pepper
- 2 cloves garlic, minced
- 3 tablespoons slivered almonds
- 3 tablespoons chopped fresh dill
- 1 (17 ounce) package frozen puff pastry, thawed
- 1 egg
- 1 teaspoon water
- 1 pinch salt

Direction

- Start preheating the oven to 375°F (190°C). Use cooking spray to spray the sides and bottom of a 9x13" baking pan.
- In a big bowl, mix together dill, almonds, garlic, red bell pepper, onion, broccoli, mayonnaise, Mexican cheese blend, and chicken.
- On a surface scattered with flour, roll the pastry sheets until all sides are longer than the bottom of the prepared pan by 3 inches. Put 1 sheet against the sides and on the bottom of the pan. Put the chicken filling evenly on the bottom crust. Put the second crust on top, tucking the ends between the bottom crust and the pan. Pinch crusts together to fasten.
- In a bowl, whisk eggs with salt and water, brush the top crust with this mixture. Slit vents into the top to release the steam.
- Put in the preheated oven and bake for 30 minutes until the top turns golden brown.

Nutrition Information

- Calories: 611 calories;
- Total Carbohydrate: 21.2 g
- Cholesterol: 96 mg
- Total Fat: 46.8 g
- Protein: 26.3 g
- Sodium: 411 mg

128. Quick Poached Salmon With Dill Mustard Sauce

""This salmon dish is simple enough to make with its elegant no-cook sauce. Preparing it doesn't get any easier. It's great for those particularly hot summer days with some freshly steamed asparagus, and the nice combination of the sauce.""

Serving: 4 | Prep: 15m | Ready in: 30m

Ingredients

- 1/2 cup plain yogurt
- 1/4 cup Dijon mustard
- 1 tablespoon honey
- 1/4 cup fresh lemon juice
- 3 tablespoons chopped fresh dill
- 1 pound salmon
- 1 cup white wine
- 1/2 cup water
- 1/4 cup chopped shallots

Direction

- Combine the Dijon mustard, plain yogurt, honey, dill, and lemon juice in a small bowl. Cover and place in the fridge until serving.
- Set the heat to medium, then place the salmon in a medium saucepan with white wine and water. Pour enough water so it just covers the fish. Add on some shallots. Cook for 10 to 12 minutes with the cover on. Check if salmon flakes easily with a fork. Drain the water and serve along with the yogurt mixture.

Nutrition Information

- Calories: 322 calories;
- Total Carbohydrate: 14.4 g
- Cholesterol: 69 mg
- Total Fat: 12.8 g
- Protein: 24.7 g
- Sodium: 470 mg

129. Quick Vegetarian Egg-lemon Soup With Brown Rice

"This is a simple but healthy vegetarian egg and lemon soup. You can make it thicker by adding another 1/2 cup rice. If you are not vegetarian, you can add in a few sautéed shrimp."

Serving: 6 | Prep: 5m | Ready in: 23m

Ingredients

- 8 cups vegetable broth
- 1 cup uncooked instant brown rice (such as Minute®)
- 6 eggs
- 1/2 cup fresh lemon juice
- 1 pinch dried dill weed, or more to taste
- 1 pinch granulated garlic, or more to taste
- salt and freshly ground black pepper to taste

Direction

- Boil broth in a big saucepan and add rice. Bring heat down and simmer, stirring sometimes, until rice becomes very tender, 10 minutes.
- In a big bowl, whisk eggs then add lemon juice. Ladle around 1 cup hot soup into the egg-lemon mixture, pour it in slowly while continuously stirring to avoid eggs from curdling.
- Stir egg mixture into the soup in the saucepan. Season with pepper, salt, garlic, and dill. Cook while stirring over low heat for 3 more minutes until eggs are cooked.

Nutrition Information

- Calories: 174 calories;
- Total Carbohydrate: 20.4 g
- Cholesterol: 186 mg
- Total Fat: 6.1 g
- Protein: 9.1 g
- Sodium: 713 mg

130. Quinoa And Dill Flatbread

""Quinoa that is good for diary-free, gluten free, vegan or vegetarian diet.""
Serving: 16 | Prep: 10m | Ready in: 30m

Ingredients

- cooking spray
- 1 1/2 cups quinoa
- 2 cups water, or more as needed
- 1/4 cup olive oil
- 2 tablespoons chopped fresh dill
- 1 tablespoon chopped fresh rosemary
- 1/2 teaspoon salt
- 1 pinch ground black pepper

Direction

- Set an oven to preheat to 175?°C (350°F). Use cooking spray to grease the two 9-inch round pans lightly.
- In a food processor, pulse the quinoa for 3-5minutes, until it is ground into flour.
- In a bowl, mix together the pepper, salt, rosemary, dill, olive oil, water and quinoa flour, then whisk, pouring in more water if necessary, until incorporated. Split the dough evenly between the prepped cake pans.
- Let it bake in the preheated oven for about 20 minutes, until the tops turn golden. Slice it into wedges.

Nutrition Information

- Calories: 89 calories;
- Total Carbohydrate: 10.3 g
- Cholesterol: 0 mg
- Total Fat: 4.4 g
- Protein: 2.3 g
- Sodium: 75 mg

131. Ranch Dressing With Fresh Herbs

"Spices and dried herbs are not used in this dressing recipe but it's packed with flavors! If you want, you may make the flavor a little more subtle. Use a mild sour cream and mild mayo instead if you want to cut down on calories. It is a great dip for vegetables or decadent foods such as chicken strips or fried onion rings. You can keep any leftovers in the fridge. You may also use plain yogurt as an alternative to sour cream but keep in mind that the taste will somewhat change."
Serving: 12 | Prep: 20m | Ready in: 2h20m

Ingredients

- 1/2 teaspoon salt
- 1 clove garlic, minced
- 2 tablespoons minced red bell pepper
- 2 green onions, minced
- 2 small shallots, minced
- 1 tablespoon minced fresh parsley leaves
- 2 teaspoons minced fresh dill
- 1 teaspoon minced fresh cilantro leaves
- 1 teaspoon fresh lemon juice
- fresh ground black pepper to taste
- 1/2 cup buttermilk
- 1/2 cup mayonnaise
- 1/4 cup sour cream

Direction

- In the bottom of a mixing bowl, put in the finely chopped garlic and salt and use the back of a spoon to mix the garlic and salt together until a pasty mixture is formed. Put in the green onion, lemon juice, red bell pepper, dill, shallot, cilantro and parsley and gently mix the mixture until thoroughly blended. Add in black pepper to taste. Put in the mayonnaise, sour cream, and buttermilk and use a wire whisk to mix the mixture until well-blended. Use a plastic wrap to cover the bowl and keep in the fridge for not less than 2 hours. You may keep the dressing mixture in the fridge for up to 1 week.

Nutrition Information

- Calories: 85 calories;
- Total Carbohydrate: 2 g
- Cholesterol: 6 mg
- Total Fat: 8.4 g
- Protein: 0.8 g
- Sodium: 163 mg

132. Refrigerator Dill Pickles

"These pickles can be enjoyed with a bun or a hotdog, or you can enjoy it alone as a tasty and healthy snack. You can store the pickles for 6 weeks."
Serving: 12 | Prep: 10m | Ready in: 3days25m

Ingredients

- 3 1/2 cups water
- 1 1/4 cups white vinegar
- 1 tablespoon sugar
- 1 tablespoon sea salt
- 4 cups cucumber spears
- 2 cloves garlic, whole
- 2 heads fresh dill

Direction

- In a saucepan, mix sea salt, sugar, vinegar, and water together over high heat. Boil it, take away from heat and let cool entirely.
- In a big plastic or glass container, mix together fresh dill, garlic cloves, and cucumber spears. Add the cooled vinegar mixture to the cucumber mixture. Cover the container with a lid and chill for a minimum of 3 days.

Nutrition Information

- Calories: 13 calories;
- Total Carbohydrate: 3.1 g
- Cholesterol: 0 mg
- Total Fat: 0.1 g
- Protein: 0.4 g
- Sodium: 444 mg

133. Refrigerator Garlic Dill Spears

"These dill spears are perfect to enjoy with sandwiches, or you can just chop it and enjoy it as a topping for a hot dog."
Serving: 20 | Prep: 20m | Ready in: 2days

Ingredients

- 6 cloves garlic, peeled
- 4 teaspoons dill seed
- 2 teaspoons black peppercorns
- 3 pounds kirby cucumbers (or other unwaxed, small-seeded 4- to 5-inch pickling cucumbers)
- 2 1/4 cups apple cider vinegar
- 2 1/4 cups water
- 6 3/4 teaspoons pickling salt

Direction

- Distribute peppercorns, dill, and garlic among 2 clean quart jars. Rinse cucumbers and cut off the blossom ends. Slice each cucumber into 6-8 spears. In the jars, pack the spears tightly and vertically.
- In a small nonreactive pot, combine salt, water, and vinegar, and boil over high heat. Toss and lower the heat if needed until the salt melts. Take away from heat. Ladle or pour the hot brine into the jars, submerge the cucumbers keeping 1/2" headspace. Remove any air bubbles by patting the jars. Add more brine if needed to keep 1/2" headspace. Clean the rims using a damp paper towel.
- Allow full cooling for 1 hour to room temperature. Screw on the clean lids. For the best flavors, chill for a minimum of 48 hours. (The flavor gets better with time). Preserve in the fridge for a maximum of 1 month.

Nutrition Information

- Calories: 18 calories;
- Total Carbohydrate: 3.3 g
- Cholesterol: 0 mg
- Total Fat: 0.1 g
- Protein: 0.6 g

- Sodium: 789 mg

134. Roasted Garlic & Herb Bread

"This is a quick bread that's great for beginners to make."
Serving: 12 | Ready in: 2h15m

Ingredients

- 2 heads garlic, roasted (see How To) and cooled
- 1¼ cups white whole-wheat flour (see Note)
- 1¼ cups all-purpose flour
- 2 tablespoons plus 1 teaspoon chopped fresh herbs such as rosemary, thyme, oregano and/or dill, or 2½ teaspoons dried, divided
- 1 tablespoon baking powder
- ¼ teaspoon baking soda
- ½ teaspoon salt
- ¼ teaspoon freshly ground pepper
- 2 large eggs
- 1¼ cups low-fat milk
- ⅓ cup extra-virgin olive oil

Direction

- Put rack in the center of your oven. Preheat it to 375°F. Line parchment paper on a 9x5-in. or similarly sized loaf pan. Coat paper and pan's sides generously with cooking spray.
- Peel the roasted garlic cloves and keep them whole.
- In a big bowl, whisk pepper, salt, baking soda, baking powder, 2 tbsp. fresh herbs/2 tsp. dried herbs, all-purpose flour and whole-wheat flour. In a medium bowl, whisk oil, milk and eggs. Add wet ingredients into dry ingredients. Stir gently until nearly combined. Add garlic cloves. Fold into the batter gently until combined evenly; don't overmix. Scrape batter into prepped pan. Smooth top. Sprinkle leftover 1 tsp. fresh herbs/ 1/2 tsp. dried herbs.
- Bake bread for 40-45 minutes until an inserted toothpick in the middle exits cleanly and top is lightly browned. Cool on a wire rack in pan for 15 minutes. Around and under the loaf, run a knife to loosen it. Turn out onto rack. Cool for a minimum of 30 minutes; slice. Serve at room temperature or warm.

Nutrition Information

- Calories: 179 calories;
- Total Carbohydrate: 23 g
- Cholesterol: 32 mg
- Total Fat: 7 g
- Fiber: 2 g
- Protein: 5 g
- Sodium: 270 mg
- Sugar: 1 g
- Saturated Fat: 1 g

135. Roasted Green Beans With Dill Vinaigrette

"This is my favorite recipe for every dinner. Trimmed beans helps saving your time. I normally double the recipe since beans shrink when roasted.""
Serving: 4 | Prep: 15m | Ready in: 35m

Ingredients

- 2 pounds fresh green beans, trimmed
- 1 tablespoon olive oil
- 1/2 teaspoon coarse salt
- 1 tablespoon olive oil
- 2 tablespoons red wine vinegar
- 1 1/2 teaspoons Dijon mustard
- 1 teaspoon white sugar
- 1/2 teaspoon dried dill
- 1/2 teaspoon coarse-ground black pepper

Direction

- Turn oven to 450°F (230°C) to preheat.
- In a large mixing bowl, combine coarse salt and 1 tablespoon olive oil with the green beans; stir until evenly coated.
- Roast seasoned green beans for about 20 minutes in the preheated oven until cooked through.

- In a mixing bowl, whisk together pepper, dill, sugar, Dijon mustard, red wine vinegar, and 1 tablespoon of olive oil. Drizzle dressing over the toasted green beans and serve.

Nutrition Information

- Calories: 139 calories;
- Total Carbohydrate: 18.4 g
- Cholesterol: 0 mg
- Total Fat: 7 g
- Protein: 4.2 g
- Sodium: 352 mg

136. Salmon 'tartare' Spread

"You can serve this Salmon 'Tartare' Spread on toasts, sesame crackers or kettle-style potato chips."
Serving: 10

Ingredients

- 1/4 cup capers, packed in brine and drained
- 8 ounces good-quality smoked salmon
- 2 tablespoons chopped fresh dill
- 2 tablespoons extra-virgin olive oil
- 1/2 teaspoon finely grated lemon zest
- 1/4 cup finely diced red onion

Direction

- In a food processor that is fitted with a steel blade, pulse the capers until they are coarsely chopped. Add lemon zest, oil, dill and salmon and then pulse until well-mixed and the salmon is chopped finely. Mix in the red onion. Serve together with toasts, sesame crackers or kettle-style potato chips. In case you assemble the hors d'oeuvres (instead of allowing the guests prepare their own), add a thin slice of lemon, rind and all on top of every tartare-covered toast or chip.

Nutrition Information

- Calories: 54 calories;
- Total Carbohydrate: 0.6 g
- Cholesterol: 5 mg
- Total Fat: 3.7 g
- Protein: 4.3 g
- Sodium: 280 mg

137. Salmon Bisque For Two

"A quick soup featuring salmon."
Serving: 2 | Prep: 15m | Ready in: 45m

Ingredients

- 1 tablespoon butter
- 1 tablespoon chopped yellow onion
- 1 tablespoon all-purpose flour
- 1/2 teaspoon chicken bouillon granules
- 1/2 pound salmon fillet, finely chopped
- 3/4 cup half-and-half cream, divided
- 1/4 teaspoon dill weed
- 1/8 teaspoon white pepper
- 1/8 teaspoon paprika
- 2 tablespoons port wine
- salt to taste

Direction

- In a saucepan, melt butter on medium heat. Mix onion in; cook till it starts to brown. Sprinkle bouillon granules and flour; mix till melted butter gets absorbed.
- Mix 1/2 cup of half-and-half and salmon in. Mix paprika, white pepper and dill in; cook, occasionally mixing, for 10 minutes. Take off heat; slightly cool.
- Puree salmon mixture in a food processor/blender. Put into a saucepan on medium low heat. Add leftover 1/4 cup of half-and-half slowly. Mix port in; cook for 5-7 minutes. Season to taste with salt.

Nutrition Information

- Calories: 406 calories;
- Total Carbohydrate: 8 g
- Cholesterol: 116 mg
- Total Fat: 28.6 g

- Protein: 25.9 g
- Sodium: 154 mg

138. Salmon Cakes With Olives, Lemon & Dill

"This dish is studded with a little dill, lemon zest, and briny olives. You can put a dollop of reduced-fat mayo and combine with lemon juice to enjoy with any dish."
Serving: 8 | Ready in: 30m

Ingredients

- 4 scallions, quartered
- ½ cup pitted Kalamata olives
- 3 tablespoons coarsely chopped fresh dill or thyme
- Zest of 2 lemons
- ½ teaspoon salt
- ½ teaspoon freshly ground pepper
- 2½ pounds wild salmon (see Tip), skinned and cut into 2-inch chunks
- 4 teaspoons extra-virgin olive oil, divided

Direction

- Pulse dill (or thyme), olives, and scallions in a food processor until finely chopped. Move to a big bowl. Mix in pepper, salt, and lemon zest.
- Divide into 3-4 batches, pulse salmon twice or thrice to finely chop, but not puree. Add it to the bowl; lightly toss until blended. (Alternatively, you can cut the herbs, olives, scallions, and salmon finely by hands, and then mix with pepper, salt, and lemon zest). Distribute the mixture into 8 patties, approximately 3/4-inch thick and 3-inch wide. Refrigerate in the fridge for a minimum of 20 minutes (or a maximum of 2 hours), and then start cooking.
- In a big nonstick frying pan, heat 2 teaspoons oil over medium heat. Add 4 salmon cakes and cook for 6-8 minutes total until just thoroughly cooked and both sides turn brown. Do the same with the left salmon cakes and oil.

Nutrition Information

- Calories: 214 calories;
- Total Carbohydrate: 2 g
- Cholesterol: 66 mg
- Total Fat: 10 g
- Fiber: 1 g
- Protein: 29 g
- Sodium: 339 mg
- Sugar: 0 g
- Saturated Fat: 2 g

139. Salmon Dill Biscuits

"You can serve these appetizers in festive baking cups and it's perfect to serve at any parties."
Serving: 12 | Prep: 20m | Ready in: 40m

Ingredients

- 12 Reynolds® StayBrite® Baking Cups
- 2 cups all-purpose flour
- 1 tablespoon sugar
- 1 1/2 teaspoons baking powder
- 1/2 teaspoon baking soda
- 1/2 teaspoon salt
- 1 cup buttermilk
- 2 eggs
- 1/4 cup butter, melted
- 2 tablespoons snipped fresh dill plus additional for serving
- 4 ounces smoked salmon (lox-style), divided
- 1/2 cup whipped cream cheese, softened

Direction

- Start preheating the oven to 400°F. Use 12 Reynolds(R) Foil Baking Cups to line a muffin pan, put aside. Combine salt, baking soda, baking powder, sugar, and flour in a big bowl. Create a well in the middle of the flour mixture and put aside.
- In a 2-cup measure, combine dill, butter, eggs, buttermilk. Add all at the same time to the flour mixture. Lightly mix until damped (the

batter will not be lumpy). Cut 2 ounces of the smoked salmon. Carefully fold in salmon.
- Put the batter into the prepared muffin cups; put three-fourths full in each to fill.
- Put in the preheated oven and bake until turning golden, about 15 minutes. Put the cups on a wire rack to let it cool down, about 5 minutes.
- Cut the muffins into two and use cream cheese to spread on the cut side. Insert some of the rest 2 ounces smoked salmon between muffin halves. Use more fresh dill to garnish.

Nutrition Information

- Calories: 166 calories;
- Total Carbohydrate: 18.5 g
- Cholesterol: 51 mg
- Total Fat: 7.6 g
- Protein: 6 g
- Sodium: 377 mg

140. Salmon En Papillote

"This salmon dish is healthy, tasty, and very easy to make."
Serving: 4 | Prep: 10m | Ready in: 33m

Ingredients

- 4 (5 ounce) salmon fillets
- salt and freshly ground black pepper to taste
- 2 tablespoons olive oil
- 2 tablespoons balsamic vinegar
- 2 sprigs fresh dill, stemmed
- 4 slices lemon
- 1/2 (8 ounce) container creme fraiche
- 1 lemon, juiced

Direction

- Start preheating the oven to 400°F (200°C).
- Slice a big page of aluminum foil into four square pieces, about 8 inches each piece. On each piece, put 1 salmon fillet, use pepper and salt to season. Drizzle the fillet with balsamic vinegar and olive oil. Use dill fronds to sprinkle on top. Put on each fillet 1 lemon slice.
- To make packets around the salmon fillets, raise the ends of aluminum foil and fold together. Move the packets to a cookie sheet.
- Put in the preheated oven and bake for 20 minutes until a fork can easily flake the fish.
- In a small saucepan, mix together pepper, salt, lemon juice, and creme fraiche over low heat. Toss for 3-5 minutes until the sauce is thoroughly heated.
- Gently open the foil packets. Put over the salmon the sauce.

Nutrition Information

- Calories: 376 calories;
- Total Carbohydrate: 6.5 g
- Cholesterol: 103 mg
- Total Fat: 26.2 g
- Protein: 31.8 g
- Sodium: 111 mg

141. Salmon Fillets With Creamy Dill

"This is family recipe for how Alaskans prepare a tasty salmon dish. You can use silver, king or red salmon. You can serve together with wild rice!"
Serving: 4 | Prep: 5m | Ready in: 45m

Ingredients

- 1 1/2 cups mayonnaise
- 1/2 cup prepared mustard
- 1 teaspoon chopped fresh thyme
- 1 teaspoon dried oregano
- 1 teaspoon chopped fresh basil leaves
- 1 1/2 pounds salmon fillets
- 2 teaspoons dried dill, or to taste

Direction

- Preheat an oven to 190 degrees C (375 degrees F).

- Mix together mustard and mayonnaise in a bowl. Mix in basil, thyme, and oregano. Put the salmon fillets onto a baking sheet and then brush with mayonnaise mixture. Drizzle dill weed on top.
- Bake for about 30 to 40 minutes until salmon flakes easily with a fork.

Nutrition Information

- Calories: 861 calories;
- Total Carbohydrate: 4.8 g
- Cholesterol: 107 mg
- Total Fat: 76.8 g
- Protein: 38.6 g
- Sodium: 895 mg

142. Salmon Patties With Dill Sauce

"Bond with your kids over these healthy salmon patties made with mayo."
Serving: 2 | Prep: 20m | Ready in: 30m

Ingredients

- Salmon Patties:
- 1 (5 ounce) can salmon, drained and flaked
- 1/2 cup dried breadcrumbs
- 2 tablespoons minced onion
- 1 tablespoon Dijon mustard
- 1 egg, lightly beaten
- 1 teaspoon lemon juice
- sea salt and ground black pepper to taste
- 1 tablespoon olive oil, or as needed
- Dill Sauce:
- 1/4 cup light sour cream
- 1 teaspoon dill weed
- 1/4 teaspoon garlic powder
- sea salt to taste

Direction

- In a bowl, combine salmon, breadcrumbs, egg, onion, lemon juice, and Dijon mustard. Create 2 patties from the mixture.
- On medium-high heat, heat olive oil in a skillet. Fry patties for 4 minutes on each side, until lightly browned and cooked through. Season with black pepper and sea salt.
- In a bowl, mix together the garlic powder, sea salt, dill, and sour cream. Serve the mixture with the patties.

Nutrition Information

- Calories: 376 calories;
- Total Carbohydrate: 24.2 g
- Cholesterol: 136 mg
- Total Fat: 19.5 g
- Protein: 24.5 g
- Sodium: 1010 mg

143. Salmon Salad

"You can replace the standard tuna salad with this salmon salad."
Serving: 4 | Prep: 5m | Ready in: 5m

Ingredients

- 2 (7 ounce) cans salmon, drained
- 2 tablespoons fat-free mayonnaise
- 2 tablespoons plain low-fat yogurt
- 1 cup chopped celery
- 2 tablespoons capers
- 1/8 teaspoon ground black pepper
- 8 leaves lettuce

Direction

- In a 1 quart bowl, crumble the salmon and remove any bones or skin.
- Mix the capers, celery, pepper, mayonnaise, and yogurt in a small bowl. Combine thoroughly and transfer to bowl of salmon and mix. You can serve atop a bed of lettuce leaves.

Nutrition Information

- Calories: 182 calories;
- Total Carbohydrate: 3.7 g

- Cholesterol: 44 mg
- Total Fat: 7.4 g
- Protein: 23.9 g
- Sodium: 568 mg

144. Salmon With Creamy Dill Sauce From Swanson®

""This dish is such an elegant hit that will impress your guests.""
Serving: 4 | Prep: 15m | Ready in: 50m

Ingredients

- 4 (5 ounce) salmon fillets, skin removed
- 1/8 teaspoon salt
- 1/8 teaspoon ground black pepper
- 2 tablespoons olive oil
- 1/4 cup minced shallot
- 1 clove garlic, minced
- 1/4 cup dry white wine
- 1 cup Swanson® Seafood Stock
- 1/4 cup heavy cream
- 1 tablespoon chopped fresh dill weed

Direction

- Sprinkle black pepper and salt over fish to season.
- In a 10-inch skillet, heat 1 tablespoon oil over medium-high heat. Add fish to the heated oil and cook for 3 minutes. Flip over and cook for 1 more minute. Take fish out of the skillet. Clean the skillet with a paper towel.
- Also in this skillet, heat the remaining oil over medium-high heat. Stir-fry garlic and shallots in hot oil until softened, about 3 minutes.
- Mix in the wine and cook until liquid is nearly vaporized, about 3 minutes. Mix in heavy cream and stock, bring to a boil. Lower heat to medium. Cook, stirring frequently, until mixture is reduced to approximately 3/4 cup, about 15 minutes. Add dill and mix well.
- Bring fish back to the skillet. Put the lid on and cook until fish flakes easily with a fork, about 5 minutes.

Nutrition Information

- Calories: 395 calories;
- Total Carbohydrate: 3.1 g
- Cholesterol: 104 mg
- Total Fat: 27.7 g
- Protein: 29.2 g
- Sodium: 302 mg

145. Salmon With Lemon And Dill

"This amazing recipe belongs to my Aunt. The fish tastes more delicious with dill and lemon. I prefer to use Alaskan salmon for this dish, but any other kinds of salmon work great as well."
Serving: 4 | Prep: 10m | Ready in: 35m

Ingredients

- 1 pound salmon fillets
- 1/4 cup butter, melted
- 5 tablespoons lemon juice
- 1 tablespoon dried dill weed
- 1/4 teaspoon garlic powder
- sea salt to taste
- freshly ground black pepper to taste

Direction

- Start preheating the oven to 350°F (175°C). Lightly oil a medium-sized baking plate.
- In the baking plate, put the salmon. In a small bowl, combine lemon juice and butter, and sprinkle over the salmon. Use pepper, sea salt, garlic powder, and dill to season.
- Put in the preheated oven and bake for 25 minutes until a fork can easily flake the salmon.

Nutrition Information

- Calories: 320 calories;
- Total Carbohydrate: 2.4 g
- Cholesterol: 104 mg
- Total Fat: 22.1 g
- Protein: 25.7 g
- Sodium: 197 mg

146. Salmon, Cream Cheese & Dill Souffle

"This salmon and dill soufflé has a rich flavor from reduced-fat cream cheese. Enjoy this dish with salad for a light supper.""
Serving: 8 | Ready in: 1h15m

Ingredients

- 3 tablespoons fine, dry breadcrumbs
- 1½ cups low-fat milk
- 2 tablespoons unsalted butter
- 2 tablespoons canola oil
- ¼ cup white whole-wheat flour (see Tips) or all-purpose flour
- 4 large egg yolks, at room temperature (see Tips)
- 4 ounces reduced-fat cream cheese (Neufchâtel), softened
- 4 ounces smoked salmon, chopped
- 2 tablespoons chopped fresh dill or 2 teaspoons dried
- ¼ teaspoon freshly ground pepper
- 8 large egg whites, at room temperature (see Tips)
- ⅛ teaspoon salt

Direction

- Turn oven to 375°F to preheat, placing rack in the lower third of the oven. Grease a 2 1/2-quart soufflé dish (or similar-size baking dish) or eight 10-ounce ramekins with cooking spray. Sprinkle with breadcrumbs and tilt until the inside is liberally and evenly coated; gently tap to remove excess. Arrange ramekins on a baking sheet.
- In a small saucepan, heat milk over medium heat until steaming. In a medium saucepan, heat oil and butter over medium-low heat. Mix in flour, cook, whisking well for 2 minutes. Add hot milk, stirring slowly; cook while stirring over medium-low heat for 2 to 4 minutes until the mixture reaches the desired batter consistency. Pour mixture into a large bowl, add egg yolks, one at a time, whisking well after each addition until incorporated. Pour in cream cheese whisking until melted, then mix in pepper, dill, and salmon.
- Clean beaters and a large mixing bowl, dry them carefully and make sure that no oil remains. (Any fat in the egg whites may prevent the rising process of your soufflé). In a mixing bowl, beat egg whites with an electric mixer on medium speed until foamy. Sprinkle with salt and, slowly increase the speed to high and beat until stiff and shiny, but not dry (avoid overbeating). Stop beating once egg whites remain their shape in the bowl and on the beater; it shouldn't be overly lumpy and dry.
- Stir 1/3 egg whites into the egg yolk mixture with a rubber spatula in order to lighten the yolk mixture. Fold in the rest of egg whites gently until evenly distributed. It's still ok if just a few white stripes remain. Ladle the batter into the prepared dish or ramekins.
- Bake in the preheated oven until puff and firm when touching, 38 to 42 minutes for a 2 1/2-quart soufflé and 20 to 24 minutes for the ramekins. (Do not open the oven door until the last 5 minutes of baking time to prevent interrupting the rising process). Even a beautifully puffed soufflé will slowly deflate once out of the oven, so quickly bring it to the table and serve right away.

Nutrition Information

- Calories: 192 calories;
- Total Carbohydrate: 7 g
- Cholesterol: 116 mg
- Total Fat: 13 g
- Fiber: 1 g
- Protein: 11 g
- Sodium: 261 mg
- Sugar: 3 g
- Saturated Fat: 5 g

147. Savory Lemon Dill Parmesan Scones

"This recipe for scone is savory but it's not super-rich. I like because I made it with the ingredients that are always available in the house. They are a great addition to breakfast/brunch/lunch, for a snack or as a side along with dinner (fish or poultry would be a great companion). They are great for entertaining when prepare more than one batch at a time."

Serving: 8 | Prep: 30m | Ready in: 55m

Ingredients

- Mock Buttermilk:
- 1/2 teaspoon lemon juice
- 1/2 cup soy milk
- Scones:
- 2 cups all-purpose flour
- 5 tablespoons lemon juice, divided
- 1 tablespoon white sugar
- 2 1/2 teaspoons baking powder
- 2 teaspoons dried dill
- 3/4 teaspoon salt
- 1/2 cup chilled unsalted butter, cut into pieces
- 1 egg
- Topping:
- 1 egg, beaten
- 1/4 cup grated Parmesan cheese
- 1 teaspoon ground black pepper

Direction

- Preheat the oven to 190 degrees C (375 degrees F). Line parchment paper onto a baking sheet.
- In a small bowl, mix 1/2 teaspoon of lemon juice in the soy milk to form mock buttermilk. Allow to stand for 5 to 10 minutes until curdled.
- Use a fork to combine flour, sugar, baking powder, salt, dill, and 3 tablespoons of lemon juice together in a big bowl. Use a pastry blender to stir in butter until the dough begins to clump together.
- In a bowl, whisk together egg, leftover 2 tablespoons lemon juice and mock buttermilk. Spread on the dough and gently stir with a fork until incorporated.
- Lightly dust the work surface using flour. Flip the dough out and then pat to form an 8-inch disc. Roll in half and flatten gently back out into a disc. Repeat rolling and flattening dough for another three times to generate fluffy layers in dough.
- Place disc of dough on the baking sheet and rub with beaten egg. Chop in 8 wedges and then pull the wedges apart so that they're not touching.
- Bake for 10 minutes until they become golden lightly.
- Take out the scones from the oven. In a small bowl, mix together black pepper and Parmesan cheese. Drizzle over the scones.
- Place back in the oven and then bake for another 10 minutes until turned golden brown and the edges appear dry.

Nutrition Information

- Calories: 263 calories;
- Total Carbohydrate: 28.1 g
- Cholesterol: 79 mg
- Total Fat: 14.1 g
- Protein: 6.5 g
- Sodium: 437 mg

148. Shrimp And Dill Deviled Eggs

"This dish has a twist that is dill and shrimp. You can use dried dill instead of the fresh one."

Serving: 12 | Prep: 40m | Ready in: 50m

Ingredients

- 6 eggs
- 1/4 cup mayonnaise
- 1 (4.5 ounce) can shrimp, rinsed and drained
- 2 tablespoons chopped green onions
- 1 tablespoon chopped fresh dill weed
- 1 tablespoon lime juice
- 2 teaspoons prepared Dijon-style mustard
- 1/4 teaspoon hot pepper sauce

- 1 pinch ground black pepper
- fresh dill weed

Direction

- In a medium-sized saucepan, put eggs and cover with cold water. Boil the water and immediately take away from heat. Put the lid on and let eggs stay in hot water for 10-12 minutes. Take out of the hot water, let cool down and remove the shells.
- Cut the eggs into two lengthwise. Scoop out the yolks. Put the egg whites aside.
- Use a fork to crush the egg yolks in a medium-sized bowl. Combine with ground black pepper, hot pepper sauce, prepared Dijon-style mustard, lime juice, fresh dill weed, green onions, shrimp, and mayonnaise.
- Use about 1 tablespoon of the egg yolk mixture to put in each egg white. Use fresh dill weed to garnish. Refrigerate in the fridge until eating.

Nutrition Information

- Calories: 83 calories;
- Total Carbohydrate: 0.9 g
- Cholesterol: 113 mg
- Total Fat: 6.3 g
- Protein: 5.7 g
- Sodium: 103 mg

149. Simple Herb Salad Mix

"This recipe is an herb salad mix. You can add dried fruit, dressings, toppings, and meats according to your liking. Just place any leftover greens inside the resealable plastic bag and store it inside the fridge for up to 2-3 days."
Serving: 5 | Prep: 20m | Ready in: 20m

Ingredients

- 1 (5 ounce) bag mesclun lettuce salad mix
- 1 (5 ounce) package baby spinach
- 1 (5 ounce) package baby arugula
- 1 small head endive, sliced
- 1/4 cup coarsely chopped parsley
- 1/4 cup coarsely chopped dill
- 1/4 cup coarsely chopped tarragon (optional)

Direction

- In a large bowl, mix the baby spinach, dill, tarragon, mesclun lettuce, parsley, endive, and baby arugula. Fold the mixture gently to mix well.
- Pour the mixture into a gallon-size resealable plastic bag. Seal and press all the air out to avoid condensation. Store the bag inside the fridge.

Nutrition Information

- Calories: 35 calories;
- Total Carbohydrate: 6 g
- Cholesterol: 0 mg
- Total Fat: 0.6 g
- Protein: 3.2 g
- Sodium: 58 mg

150. Slow-roasted Whole Salmon

"This dish is salmon filled with onions and herbs, slowly roasted in aluminum foil. You can enjoy this stuffed salmon fish on a buffet. Capers, lemon slices, and fresh herbs will be the best to garnish this dish."
Serving: 6 | Prep: 15m | Ready in: 3h

Ingredients

- 1/2 cup butter, cut into small pieces
- 1 (3 pound) whole salmon, or more to taste
- 1 onion, thinly sliced
- 1 tablespoon dried tarragon
- 1 tablespoon dried dill weed
- 3 bay leaves

Direction

- Start preheating the oven to 250°F (120°C).
- Spread out a long sheet of aluminum foil long enough to fully wrap around the fish. Use few pieces of butter to rub liberally. Put the fish on top and spread 1 thin layer of onion slices

inside the fish's cavity. Put the rest of the butter on top of the onion.
- Divide bay leaves, dill, and tarragon over the salmon. Wrap the fish loosely but securely with the aluminum foil, prevent the juices from leaking by folding seams together. Transfer the packet on a big roasting pan.
- Put in the preheated oven and bake for 2 1/2 hours until a fork can easily flake the fish.
- Take the salmon out of the oven and let sit in the aluminum foil to cool for a minimum of 15 minutes. Carefully remove the packet from the bottom of the fish and move the fish to a dish. Use a fork to carefully peel the skin off.

Nutrition Information

- Calories: 398 calories;
- Total Carbohydrate: 4.3 g
- Cholesterol: 137 mg
- Total Fat: 23 g
- Protein: 41.9 g
- Sodium: 214 mg

151. Smoked Salmon & Dill Scones

""You do not need a course for this recipe: easy to make as batch of muffins. Boosted fiber with white whole-wheat flours, and butter enough to give them perfect texture and taste without worrying the about the calories. Serve them alongside your dinner salad or brunch.""

Serving: 12 | Ready in: 45m

Ingredients

- 1½ cups all-purpose flour plus 2 tablespoons, divided
- 1¼ cups white whole-wheat flour
- 1 tablespoon plus 1 teaspoon baking powder
- 1 tablespoon sugar
- ½ teaspoon salt
- 5 tablespoons cold unsalted butter, cut into ½-inch cubes
- ⅓ cup chopped smoked salmon (2 ounces)
- ⅓ cup finely chopped red onion
- ¼ cup minced fresh dill
- 1 cup reduced-fat milk or buttermilk
- 1 large egg

Direction

- Prepare the oven by preheating to 400°F. Use cooking spray to coat a large baking sheet.
- In a large bowl, mix together the salt, sugar, baking powder, whole wheat flour, and one and a half cups all-purpose flour. Rub or slice butter into the dry ingredients using your fingertips or a pastry blender. Mix in dill, and onion and salmon.
- In a medium bowl, mix together the egg and milk or buttermilk; add into the dry ingredients until well combined.
- Drizzle 1 tablespoon flour on a work surface. And roll the dough out and drizzle the left 1 tablespoon flour on top. Massage 3 to five times, or until the dough just holds together. Split in half and dab each piece into a 5 inch circle.
- Slice each circle into 6 wedges and send to the prepared baking sheet.
- Bake the scones for 18 to 24 minutes until firm.

Nutrition Information

- Calories: 173 calories;
- Total Carbohydrate: 25 g
- Cholesterol: 31 mg
- Total Fat: 6 g
- Fiber: 2 g
- Protein: 5 g
- Sodium: 302 mg
- Sugar: 2 g
- Saturated Fat: 3 g

152. Smoked Salmon Dill Eggs Benedict

""This smoked salmon eggs benedict recipe tastes so good even without the traditional hollandaise sauce.""
Serving: 2 | Prep: 10m | Ready in: 20m

Ingredients

- 1/4 cup butter, softened
- 2 tablespoons fresh dill
- 1 teaspoon lemon zest
- 1 pinch cayenne pepper
- salt and ground black pepper to taste
- 1 teaspoon white vinegar
- 1 pinch salt
- 4 eggs
- 2 English muffins, split and toasted
- 4 ounces sliced smoked salmon
- 1 pinch cayenne pepper
- salt and ground black pepper to taste
- 4 small fresh dill sprigs

Direction

- Take a bowl and mix black pepper, salt, cayenne pepper, lemon zest, dill and butter until combined then set aside.
- Take a big saucepan and fill with 2-3 inches of water. Let it boil on high heat. Lower the heat to medium low then pour vinegar in and a little salt. In a bowl, crack one egg and slowly transfer to water. Repeat the process with the rest of the eggs. Continue poaching eggs until yolks are thick but not yet hard and whites become firm, 4-6 minutes. Use slotted spoon to remove eggs from the water then transfer to a warm plate. Use kitchen towel to remove excess water from the eggs.
- Spread dill butter generously on each English muffin half. Put smoked salmon on top and 1 poached egg. For added taste, sprinkle black pepper, salt and cayenne pepper on top and put a dill sprig over before serving.

Nutrition Information

- Calories: 528 calories;
- Total Carbohydrate: 27 g
- Cholesterol: 400 mg
- Total Fat: 35.3 g
- Protein: 26.3 g
- Sodium: 1298 mg

153. Smoked Salmon Spread

"This is a tasty and simple spread which often receives many compliments. Serve it smoked salmon and bland crackers to taste. If desired, add chopped capers for extra flavor. You can serve this dish onto a plate and place spread in a mold prior to serving."
Serving: 9 | Prep: 5m | Ready in: 5m

Ingredients

- 2 (8 ounce) packages cream cheese, softened
- 12 ounces smoked salmon, chopped
- 3 dashes Worcestershire sauce
- 3 drops hot pepper sauce
- 1 teaspoon chopped fresh dill weed
- 2 tablespoons chopped green onion

Direction

- Mix cream cheese in a medium bowl until no longer a hard form. Add dill, salmon, onion, Worcestershire sauce, and hot pepper sauce and combine thoroughly before serving.

Nutrition Information

- Calories: 219 calories;
- Total Carbohydrate: 1.5 g
- Cholesterol: 63 mg
- Total Fat: 19 g
- Protein: 10.7 g
- Sodium: 453 mg

154. Smoked Trout Salad With Herb & Horseradish Dressing

"This appetizing salad is lovely and so yummy with watercress and mixed greens combined with creamy horseradish dressing."
Serving: 4 | Ready in: 20m

Ingredients

- Herb & Horseradish Dressing
- ½ cup crème fraÀ®che or reduced-fat sour cream (see Tips)
- ⅓ cup finely chopped mixed fresh herbs, including chives, dill, flat-leaf parsley
- 2 tablespoons prepared horseradish
- ⅛ teaspoon salt
- Freshly ground pepper to taste
- Smoked Trout Salad
- 1 head butterhead lettuce, torn into bite-size pieces
- 4 cups bite-size pieces watercress or arugula (about 1 bunch), tough stems removed
- 1 cup mâche (see Tips) or mixed salad greens
- 4 ounces smoked trout fillet, skin removed
- 4 scallions, sliced
- 1 tablespoon capers, rinsed (optional)

Direction

- For dressing: Whisk together pepper, salt, horseradish, herbs, creme fraiche (or sour cream) in a small mixing bowl until incorporated.
- For salad: In a large mixing bowl, combine mache (or mixed greens), watercress (or arugula), and lettuce. Add Herbs and Horseradish Dressing and stir until evenly coated. Divide salad evenly among 4 servings. Flake each serving with 1 ounce of trout and sprinkle with capers and scallions, if desired.

Nutrition Information

- Calories: 173 calories;
- Total Carbohydrate: 4 g
- Cholesterol: 30 mg
- Total Fat: 13 g
- Fiber: 2 g
- Protein: 10 g
- Sodium: 437 mg
- Sugar: 2 g
- Saturated Fat: 7 g

155. Sour Cream, Cucumber And Dill Dip

""This dips goes really well with fish, fresh bread, chips, and even with Mediterranean food.""
Serving: 12 | Prep: 15m | Ready in: 15m

Ingredients

- 1 (16 ounce) container sour cream
- 1 cucumber, peeled, grated and squeezed as dry as possible
- 1 cup fresh dill, chopped
- 1/4 cup lemon juice, or to taste
- 1 teaspoon salt, or to taste

Direction

- In a mixing bowl, stir dill, cucumber, and sour cream together until well incorporated. Mix in salt and lemon juice. Adjust seasonings for your own taste. Chill, covered, for 1 to 2 hours.

Nutrition Information

- Calories: 86 calories;
- Total Carbohydrate: 2.8 g
- Cholesterol: 17 mg
- Total Fat: 8 g
- Protein: 1.4 g
- Sodium: 216 mg

156. Southern Dill Potato Salad

""This salad was made by my mom when I was a little boy. I've upgraded it a bit. It needs to be chilled in the fridge overnight to get the perfect flavor.""
Serving: 8 | Prep: 20m | Ready in: 1h10m

Ingredients

- 10 unpeeled red potatoes
- 5 hard boiled eggs, roughly chopped
- 3/4 cup sour cream
- 3/4 cup mayonnaise
- 1 tablespoon apple cider vinegar, or to taste
- 1 tablespoon Dijon mustard, or to taste
- 1/2 white onion, finely chopped
- 1 stalk celery, finely chopped
- 1 teaspoon celery salt
- salt and black pepper to taste
- 1 tablespoon dried dill weed

Direction

- In a large pot, pour water to cover potatoes, and boil over high heat. Lower the heat to medium-low, and simmer the potatoes for about 20 minutes until thoroughly cooked, but still firm. Drain off the water, allow to cool, and chop the potatoes into chunks. Put the chopped potatoes to one side.
- Combine pepper, salt, celery salt, celery, onion, Dijon mustard, apple cider vinegar, mayonnaise, and sour cream in a bowl until well incorporated.
- In a large salad bowl, put eggs and potatoes, sprinkle with some dried dill. Pour the dressing mixture over the eggs and potatoes, toss gently. Chilled while covered for 30 minutes or more, and serve cold.

Nutrition Information

- Calories: 279 calories;
- Total Carbohydrate: 10.8 g
- Cholesterol: 134 mg
- Total Fat: 24.1 g
- Protein: 5.9 g
- Sodium: 413 mg

157. Spicy Refrigerator Dill Pickles

"This tasty pickle is a little sweet. If you really like spicy food, you can double the amount of crushed red pepper."
Serving: 12 | Prep: 15m | Ready in: 10days2h15m

Ingredients

- 12 3 to 4 inch long pickling cucumbers
- 2 cups water
- 1 3/4 cups white vinegar
- 1 1/2 cups chopped fresh dill weed
- 1/2 cup white sugar
- 8 cloves garlic, chopped
- 1 1/2 tablespoons coarse salt
- 1 tablespoon pickling spice
- 1 1/2 teaspoons dill seed
- 1/2 teaspoon red pepper flakes, or to taste
- 4 sprigs fresh dill weed

Direction

- Mix red pepper flakes, dill seed, pickling spice, salt, garlic, sugar, chopped dill, vinegar, water, and cucumbers together in a big bowl. Mix, and let sit at room temperature until salt and sugar melt, about 2 hours.
- Transfer the cucumbers to three 1 1/2-pint jars with wide mouths. Put into each jar 4 cucumbers. Spoon in the liquid from the bowl to fill. Put into each jar a sprig of fresh dill, then close the lids to seal. Chill for 10 days before serving. Use no longer than 1 month.

Nutrition Information

- Calories: 70 calories;
- Total Carbohydrate: 16.9 g
- Cholesterol: 0 mg
- Total Fat: 0.3 g
- Protein: 1.6 g
- Sodium: 728 mg

158. Spicy Shrimp And Red Bean Soup

""The appearance and flavor of this soup that was super simple to prepare makes it look like a fine-dining dish from a restaurant. As wonderfully as it is, it was actually the result of a mishap!""
Serving: 4 | Prep: 20m | Ready in: 40m

Ingredients

- 2 tablespoons olive oil
- 3 cloves garlic, chopped
- 1 medium celery rib, chopped
- 2 green onions, chopped
- 1 (15 ounce) can red kidney beans, drained
- 1 (10 ounce) can tomatoes with green chilies
- 1 (10 ounce) can condensed cream of mushroom soup
- 3/4 cup water
- 1 sprig fresh dill
- 12 ounces medium shrimp - peeled and deveined

Direction

- At moderate heat, heat the oil in a big saucepan. Insert the green onions, celery and garlic. Cook for around 3 minutes until the contents become tender. During the process, stir regularly. Pour in water, cream of mushroom soup, tomatoes and beans. Let the mixture come to a boil. Mix in the dill then lower the heat to medium. Leave it simmering for 10 minutes before stirring in the shrimp. Leave the shrimp simmering for around 5 minutes until they turn pink.

Nutrition Information

- Calories: 316 calories;
- Total Carbohydrate: 25.8 g
- Cholesterol: 128 mg
- Total Fat: 12.9 g
- Protein: 24.7 g
- Sodium: 1099 mg

159. Spinach With Chickpeas And Fresh Dill

"This recipe is full of flavor and is great as a dish."
Serving: 6 | Prep: 15m | Ready in: 30m

Ingredients

- 2 tablespoons olive oil
- 1 large onion, thinly sliced
- 1 1/2 cups canned chickpeas, drained
- 1 pound spinach
- 1/2 cup minced fresh dill weed
- 2 lemons, juiced
- salt and pepper to taste

Direction

- Heat olive oil in a big skillet over medium heat. Put in onion then sauté until it becomes soft. Put in chickpeas then toss to coat with oil.
- Clean the spinach well and remove thick stems. Put undrained spinach and dill into the skillet. Cook until it becomes tender.
- Mix in lemon juice. Season it with pepper and salt to taste. Serve while warm.

Nutrition Information

- Calories: 142 calories;
- Total Carbohydrate: 20.3 g
- Cholesterol: 0 mg
- Total Fat: 6 g
- Protein: 6.6 g
- Sodium: 163 mg

160. Stuffed Bell Pepper Rings

"Using pepper rings to substitute whole peppers will shorten the cooking time. When you taste it, you will taste more meat than peppers. Enjoy the dish with nonfat yogurt, Greek-style sour cream, and sour cream."
Serving: 6 | Prep: 25m | Ready in: 1h15m

Ingredients

- 2 pounds ground beef sirloin

- 1 cup cooked rice
- 1 onion, diced
- 2 eggs
- 1/2 cup cooked corn
- 1 carrot, shredded
- 3 tablespoons olive oil, divided
- 2 tablespoons Italian-seasoned bread crumbs
- 1 tablespoon sun-dried tomato pesto
- 1 tablespoon minced fresh parsley
- 2 tablespoons chopped fresh dill, divided
- 1 clove garlic, minced
- salt and ground black pepper to taste
- 4 large yellow bell peppers - tops removed, sliced into 2-inch rings, seeded, or to taste
- 2 tomatoes, sliced, or to taste
- 1/2 cup pasta sauce
- 1/2 cup chicken broth
- 3 green onions, thinly sliced, or to taste

Direction

- Start preheating the oven to 350°F (175°C).
- In a big bowl, mix together black pepper, salt, garlic, 1 tablespoon dill, parsley, pesto, bread crumbs, 1 tablespoon olive oil, carrot, corn, eggs, onion, rice, and ground beef.
- Cut any left pieces of yellow bell pepper and put them in a baking plate's bottom. Add the left dill, green onions, chicken broth, pasta sauce, tomatoes, and the left olive oil.
- In the baking plate, put the yellow bell pepper rings and use the beef-rice mixture to fill. Cover with the pasta sauce mixture on top. Use aluminum foil to cover the baking plate.
- Put in the preheated oven and bake for 30 minutes. Take away the aluminum foil and keep baking for another 20 minutes until the peppers are still tender-crisp and the beef turns brown.

Nutrition Information

- Calories: 408 calories;
- Total Carbohydrate: 27.9 g
- Cholesterol: 128 mg
- Total Fat: 18.8 g
- Protein: 32.4 g
- Sodium: 361 mg

161. Summer Cucumber Salad

"This recipe belongs to my mother and it's been a must-have at every of our meal. This also is a good way to use up cucumbers when they're in season."
Serving: 4 | Prep: 10m | Ready in: 40m

Ingredients

- 2 tablespoons chopped fresh dill
- 2 tablespoons chopped fresh chives
- 1 (8 ounce) container reduced-fat sour cream
- 1 tablespoon fresh lemon juice
- 1 large English cucumber, sliced

Direction

- In a small bowl, combine sour cream, chives, and dill. Mix lemon juice into the sour cream mixture; let it sit for 30 minutes at room temperature.
- In a big bowl, put the cucumber slices. Put the sour cream mixture on the cucumbers and lightly toss until evenly combined. Enjoy immediately.

Nutrition Information

- Calories: 87 calories;
- Total Carbohydrate: 4.7 g
- Cholesterol: 22 mg
- Total Fat: 6.8 g
- Protein: 2.7 g
- Sodium: 24 mg

162. Sweet And Sour Cabbage Soup

"A healthier version of an old favorite Ashkenazi Jewish recipe."
Serving: 12 | Prep: 1h30m | Ready in: 1day7h

Ingredients

- For the stock:

- 4 pounds bone-in beef shank
- 12 cups water
- 3 carrots, peeled and cut into 3-inch pieces
- 3 onions, peeled
- 4 stalks celery with leaves
- 1 bay leaf
- 16 peppercorns
- For the soup:
- 2 tablespoons vegetable oil
- 1 onion, peeled and diced
- 2 cloves garlic, minced
- 1 tablespoon sweet Hungarian paprika
- 1 head Savoy cabbage, coarsely chopped
- 1 (14.5 ounce) can diced tomatoes with juice
- 1 lemon, juiced
- 1/4 cup white sugar
- 1/4 cup chopped fresh dill
- salt and freshly ground black pepper to taste

Direction

- In a big stock pot, mix water and beef shanks. Boil and lower heat to a really low simmer. Remove any froth on surface with a strainer. Put peppercorns, bay leaf, celery stalks, whole onions and carrot pieces. Let simmer for 4 hours, skimming the surface from time to time.
- Drain the stock. Throw vegetables yet set the meat aside. Cool the stock to room temperature, then put to a container with cover and chill for overnight. Once beef shanks are cool, take meat off from bones. Throw the bones and gristle. Into small cubes, chop meat and any leftover marrow. Put cover on the container and chill overnight.
- The following day, in a stock pot or Dutch oven, heat vegetable oil over medium heat. Mix in 1 diced onion and garlic; allow to cook and mix for 5 minutes till onion has turned translucent and softened. Put paprika and cook for a minute longer, mixing continuously. Slowly put cabbage and allow to cook for 8 minutes, mixing from time to time, till reduced in bulk and wilted slightly.
- From the refrigerator, take the beef stock off; remove and throw any fat. Into the pot, put the stock; mix in the leftover chopped beef. Put tomatoes along with juice. Boil the soup, and lower heat to a simmer. Partly cover and allow the soup to cook for an hour, till cabbage is lightly tender.
- Stir in the lemon juice, sugar, dill, salt, and pepper. For a thinner soup, put additional water if wished. Allow to cook for 5 minutes without cover. Taste and adjust the taste prior serving.

Nutrition Information

- Calories: 247 calories;
- Total Carbohydrate: 22.3 g
- Cholesterol: 52 mg
- Total Fat: 6.9 g
- Protein: 25.3 g
- Sodium: 146 mg

163. Sweet Pea And Dill Salad

"This is a refreshing salad with fragrant dressing and sweet peas."
Serving: 4 | Prep: 10m | Ready in: 2h20m

Ingredients

- 4 cups blanched green peas
- 1/2 cup mayonnaise
- 1/2 cup sour cream
- 2 tablespoons prepared horseradish
- 1 tablespoon Dijon-style prepared mustard
- 1/4 cup chopped fresh dill weed
- ground black pepper to taste

Direction

- Use a paper towel to pat peas gently to absorb excess moisture then put into a big bowl.
- Mix together 3 tbsp. of dill weed, mustard, horseradish, sour cream and mayonnaise in a small bowl, then put the mixture into the peas and toss all together to coat. Sprinkle the leftover dill on top, then cover and refrigerate for minimum of 2 hours before serving.

Nutrition Information

- Calories: 402 calories;
- Total Carbohydrate: 28.9 g
- Cholesterol: 23 mg
- Total Fat: 28.3 g
- Protein: 9.9 g
- Sodium: 295 mg

164. Ta'ameya (Egyptian Falafel)

"In Egypt, we call this dish ta'ameya or falafel. We make this dish with dried fava beans. It's great to enjoy with tahini sauce, onions, tomato, and pita bread."
Serving: 10 | Prep: 20m | Ready in: 8h28m

Ingredients

- 2 cups dried split fava beans
- 1 red onion, quartered
- 1/2 cup fresh parsley
- 1/2 cup fresh cilantro
- 1/2 cup fresh dill
- 3 cloves garlic
- 1 1/2 teaspoons ground coriander
- 1 1/2 teaspoons salt
- 1 teaspoon ground cumin
- 1 cup sesame seeds (optional)
- vegetable oil for frying

Direction

- In a big bowl, put fava beans and fill with a few inches of water to cover. Let bath for 8 hours to overnight. Strain.
- In a food processor, mix together cumin, salt, coriander, garlic, dill, cilantro, parsley, red onion, and the soaked fava beans; blend until having a dough-liked consistency.
- Put a frying pan on medium heat. Add sesame seeds; cook, tossing sometimes, for 5 minutes until toasted. Move to a big dish.
- Form the fava bean mixture into balls. Coat the balls with sesame seeds.
- In a big saucepan, add oil until 1/4 full; heat over medium heat. Working in batches, fry the fava bean balls for 3-5 minutes until they turn golden brown. Put on paper towels to strain.

Nutrition Information

- Calories: 234 calories;
- Total Carbohydrate: 22.8 g
- Cholesterol: 0 mg
- Total Fat: 12.2 g
- Protein: 10.8 g
- Sodium: 359 mg

165. Tailgate Potato Salad

"A delicious recipe that your guests will beg for more of!"
Serving: 4 | Prep: 10m | Ready in: 1h10m

Ingredients

- 1 pound whole russet potatoes, peeled
- 3 tablespoons chicken stock
- 3 tablespoons champagne vinegar
- 3 tablespoons Sancerre or quality dry white wine
- 1/2 teaspoon minced garlic
- 1 tablespoon Dijon mustard
- 1 tablespoon kosher salt, divided
- 1 tablespoon cracked black pepper, divided
- 1/2 cup olive oil
- 2 tablespoons olive oil
- 1/2 cup green onions, chopped
- 3 tablespoons chopped fresh parsley
- 2 tablespoons chopped fresh dill
- 2 tablespoons chopped fresh basil

Direction

- In boiling water, put potatoes. Cook for about 20-30 minutes (varies based on size) until cooked thoroughly.
- Drain. Cover. Let stand until they're cool enough to the touch.
- Halve/quarter potatoes (depending on size. Smaller potatoes cook faster). Try making them uniform as possible.

- Put in a bowl with white wine and poultry stock. Mix. Let liquid absorb into the potatoes.
- Mix pepper, 1/2 of salt, Dijon mustard, vinegar and garlic well in another bowl. Whisk in 1/2 cup plus 2 tbsp. olive oil into mixture until dressing emulsifies.
- Put vinaigrette to potatoes. Mix well.
- Add basil, dill, parsley and green onions; mix again.
- Immediately serve or serve at room temperature.

Nutrition Information

- Calories: 417 calories;
- Total Carbohydrate: 25.1 g
- Cholesterol: < mg
- Total Fat: 34 g
- Protein: 3.1 g
- Sodium: 1577 mg

166. The Brutus Salad

"An amazing salad featuring Dijon vinaigrette, toasted pecans, fresh herbs, Cheddar cheese, romaine lettuce and apple slices."
Serving: 4 | Prep: 20m | Ready in: 34m

Ingredients

- Dressing:
- 1/4 cup real French Dijon mustard
- 1/4 cup seasoned rice vinegar
- 1/4 cup vegetable oil
- 1/4 teaspoon Worcestershire sauce
- freshly ground black pepper
- 1 pinch cayenne pepper, or to taste
- Toasted Pecans:
- 3/4 cup pecan halves
- 2 teaspoons vegetable oil
- 1 pinch salt, or to taste
- 1 teaspoon white sugar
- Salad:
- 4 hearts of romaine, cut or torn into bite-size pieces
- 1 apple, thinly sliced
- 2 tablespoons chopped fresh dill
- 2 tablespoons chopped fresh tarragon
- 2 ounces extra sharp aged Cheddar cheese

Direction

- In a bowl, place cayenne, pepper, Worcestershire sauce, seasoned rice vinegar, vegetable oil and Dijon mustard. Whisk thoroughly for 1 minute to blend well. Place into a container that is easy to pour.
- In a skillet, place pecans over medium heat. Drizzle vegetable oil over. Cook for 1-2 minutes till pecans have slightly darkened and smell toasty, stirring. Sprinkle sugar and kosher salt over. Cook for 1 more minute, stirring then take away from the heat. Place into a plate and let cool.
- In a large bowl, place romaine pieces. Add a handful of pecans, tarragon, dill and apple slices; save some pecans to garnish. Add grated Cheddar cheese into the salad, save some to garnish. Drizzle some dressing over and toss. Taste and season with more dressing or salt if preferred. All of the dressing may not be needed.
- Add some grated Cheddar cheese and a few toasted pecans for garnish.

Nutrition Information

- Calories: 386 calories;
- Total Carbohydrate: 14.2 g
- Cholesterol: 15 mg
- Total Fat: 35.3 g
- Protein: 6.6 g
- Sodium: 830 mg

167. Three-herb Potato Salad

"A healthy and creamy potato salad recipe."
Serving: 10 | Ready in: 45m

Ingredients

- 2½ pounds yellow or red potatoes, scrubbed and diced (½- to 1-inch)

- ¾ teaspoon salt, divided
- ½ cup mayonnaise
- ½ cup low-fat plain yogurt
- ¼ cup finely chopped onion
- 2 tablespoons Dijon mustard
- ½ teaspoon ground pepper
- 1 cup chopped mixed fresh herbs, such as parsley, dill and tarragon
- 2 scallions, sliced
- 2 tablespoons capers, rinsed

Direction

- In a big saucepan or pot fitted with a steamer basket, boil an inch to 2 inches of water. Put in potatoes, cover and allow them to cook for 12 to 15 minutes till soft. Scatter in 1 layer on a rimmed baking sheet and sprinkle with a quarter teaspoon of salt; allow it to cool for 15 minutes.
- Meantime, in a big bowl, mix together pepper, mustard, onion, yogurt, mayonnaise, and the remaining a half teaspoon of salt. Put in the capers, scallions, herbs and potatoes; mix thoroughly to coat. Serve at room temperature or chill till cold.

Nutrition Information

- Calories: 132 calories;
- Total Carbohydrate: 24 g
- Cholesterol: 3 mg
- Total Fat: 3 g
- Fiber: 2 g
- Protein: 3 g
- Sodium: 326 mg
- Sugar: 3 g
- Saturated Fat: 1 g

168. Tuna Pasta Salad With Dill

""It's an amazing dill tuna pasta salad. It's ideal for potlucks or summer parties.""
Serving: 12 | Prep: 15m | Ready in: 1h25m

Ingredients

- 1 (16 ounce) package small uncooked seashell pasta
- 1 1/2 cups mayonnaise
- 1/2 cup milk
- 2 tablespoons pickle juice
- 2 teaspoons dried dill weed
- 1 teaspoon salt
- 1/8 teaspoon ground black pepper
- 2 (5 ounce) cans tuna packed in water, drained
- 1/2 cup chopped onion (optional)

Direction

- Boil a large pot of lightly salted water. Place the pasta into the boiling water and let it cook for 8-10 minutes until al dente; drain.
- Whisk milk, pepper, mayonnaise, dill, pickle juice, and salt in a large bowl. Stir in onion and tuna. Toss the mixture with cooked pasta. Cover and refrigerate it for 1-2 hours. Serve.

Nutrition Information

- Calories: 378 calories;
- Total Carbohydrate: 30.9 g
- Cholesterol: 18 mg
- Total Fat: 23.1 g
- Protein: 11.5 g
- Sodium: 366 mg

169. Tuna Salad With Fresh Dill

"You and fill this tuna salad inside papayas or tomatoes. Very easy and delicious.""
Serving: 5 | Prep: 10m | Ready in: 10m

Ingredients

- 1 (5 ounce) can tuna

- 1/4 cup diced celery
- 1/4 cup chopped fresh dill weed
- 2 tablespoons chopped fresh parsley
- 2 tablespoons thinly sliced green onion
- 2 tablespoons fat-free mayonnaise
- 2 tablespoons plain low-fat yogurt
- 1/2 teaspoon prepared Dijon-style mustard

Direction

- Mash tuna with canned juices in a small mixing bowl. Add mustard, yogurt, mayonnaise, chives, parsley, dill, and celery into the bowl and mix until well combined.

Nutrition Information

- Calories: 41 calories;
- Total Carbohydrate: 2.3 g
- Cholesterol: 8 mg
- Total Fat: 0.3 g
- Protein: 6.9 g
- Sodium: 78 mg

170. Vegan Dill Pasta Salad

"I came up with this vegan pasta salad recipe and it's awesome.""
Serving: 8 | Prep: 25m | Ready in: 4h42m

Ingredients

- 1 (16 ounce) package fusilli pasta
- 6 large dill pickles, diced
- 1 (15 ounce) can garbanzo beans, drained and rinsed
- 1 large tomato, diced
- 3/4 cup vegan mayonnaise (such as Follow Your Heart® Veganaise®)
- 8 grape tomatoes, diced
- 1 (4.25 ounce) can minced olives
- 1/2 cup dill pickle juice
- 1/2 cup chopped fresh dill
- 1 tablespoon dried dill
- 1/2 teaspoon dry mustard

Direction

- Bring lightly salted water in a large pot to a boil. Add fusilli to boiling water, cook and stir occasionally for about 12 minutes until tender but still firm when bitten. Drain and cool until running water. Drain off water and transfer fusilli to a large bowl.
- Stir dry mustard, dried dill, fresh dill, dill pickle juice, olives grape tomatoes, vegan mayonnaise, tomato, garbanzo beans, and dill pickles into the fusilli. Chill, covered, for about 4 hours until flavors blend.

Nutrition Information

- Calories: 390 calories;
- Total Carbohydrate: 59.2 g
- Cholesterol: 0 mg
- Total Fat: 13.7 g
- Protein: 10.5 g
- Sodium: 1614 mg

171. Vegan Pasta Salad

"This is a perfect vegan pasta dish for parties with dill, tomatoes, broccoli, dill pickles and olives!"
Serving: 10 | Prep: 20m | Ready in: 3h35m

Ingredients

- 1 (16 ounce) package rotini pasta
- 1 cup chopped broccoli
- 1/2 cup vegan mayonnaise
- 1 (6 ounce) can sliced olives, drained
- 3 large dill pickles, diced
- 3 large tomatoes, diced
- 1/4 cup dill pickle juice
- 3 tablespoons minced fresh dill
- 1/2 tablespoon dried dill
- 1 teaspoon ground mustard

Direction

- Boil lightly salted water in a large pot. Cook the rotini at a boil for about 8 minutes until

tender yet firm to the bite and drain. Transfer to a large bowl.
- Add mustard, dried dill, fresh dill, pickle juice, tomatoes, pickles, olives, mayonnaise and broccoli in the bowl with the pasta and mix thoroughly to combine. Chill for at least 3 hours and stir properly before serving.

Nutrition Information

- Calories: 238 calories;
- Total Carbohydrate: 41.7 g
- Cholesterol: 3 mg
- Total Fat: 5 g
- Protein: 7.2 g
- Sodium: 854 mg

172. Vegan Ranch Dressing

""No additives needed in this creamy and vegan ranch dressing.""
Serving: 16 | Prep: 10m | Ready in: 4h10m

Ingredients

- 1 1/2 cups vegan mayonnaise (such as Follow Your Heart® Vegenaise®)
- 2 tablespoons plain soy milk, or as needed
- 1 tablespoon apple cider vinegar
- 2 teaspoons chopped fresh parsley
- 1 teaspoon garlic powder
- 1 teaspoon onion powder
- 1/2 teaspoon chopped fresh dill
- 1/4 teaspoon ground black pepper

Direction

- In a bowl, mix apple cider, soy milk, onion powder, black pepper, dill, vegan mayonnaise, parsley, and garlic powder until smooth. Cover the bowl with a plastic wrap and store it inside the refrigerator for 4 hours until the flavors are well-blended.

Nutrition Information

- Calories: 104 calories;
- Total Carbohydrate: 3.7 g
- Cholesterol: 0 mg
- Total Fat: 10.1 g
- Protein: 0.1 g
- Sodium: 76 mg

173. Walnut, Dill & Tuna Salad

"You can dress up your common tuna salad with this recipe."
Serving: 2 | Ready in: 15m

Ingredients

- 1 slice whole-grain bread
- ¼ cup reduced-sodium chicken broth
- 3 tablespoons chopped walnuts
- 2 tablespoons nonfat plain yogurt
- 2 tablespoons lemon juice
- 1 clove garlic
- Pinch of, cayenne pepper
- 1 6-ounce can chunk light tuna, drained and flaked (see Note)
- 1 carrot, chopped
- 1 stalk celery, chopped
- 2 tablespoons chopped fresh dill
- Salt & freshly ground pepper, to taste

Direction

- In a food processor, puree cayenne, garlic, lemon juice, yogurt, walnuts, broth and bread. Place in a bowl and put in dill, celery, carrot, and tuna. Use pepper and salt to season.

Nutrition Information

- Calories: 220 calories;
- Total Carbohydrate: 15 g
- Cholesterol: 31 mg
- Total Fat: 9 g
- Fiber: 4 g
- Protein: 22 g
- Sodium: 536 mg
- Sugar: 5 g
- Saturated Fat: 1 g

174. Wheat Berry Salad With Peas, Radishes, And Dill

"You can make this salad with either snow peas or sugar snap peas. Combine with radish and some dill vinaigrette, it will become a spring inside your mouth.""
Serving: 10 | Prep: 20m | Ready in: 1h25m

Ingredients

- Salad:
- 1/2 pound sugar snap peas or snow peas, trimmed
- 1 cup wheat berries, hard winter or soft wheat berries
- 1 cup frozen peas
- 4 green onions, thinly sliced
- 4 radishes, halved and thinly sliced
- Dressing:
- 2 tablespoons fresh lemon juice
- 1 teaspoon Dijon mustard
- 1 teaspoon salt
- 1 teaspoon white sugar
- 2 tablespoons extra-virgin olive oil
- 1/3 cup chopped fresh dill

Direction

- Take out the strings running along the pod of sugar snap peas. Divide each snow pea or snap pea pod into thirds diagonally.
- Bring water in a large pot to a boil over high heat. Add wheat berries, lower heat to medium, cook without a cover, stirring occasionally for about 1 hour until softened but still chewy. Mix in frozen peas and sugar snap peas and cook for 1 minute. Transfer wheat berry mixture to a large colander to drain; rinse them carefully with cold water. Drain. Remove wheat berry mixture into a large bowl and allow to cool for about 30 minutes. Mix in radishes and green onions.
- Whisk lemon juice and mustard together with sugar and salt until sugar is completely dissolved. Drizzle with oil and mix well. Pour dressing over salad and stir until evenly coated. Sprinkle with dill and stir to combine.

Nutrition Information

- Calories: 115 calories;
- Total Carbohydrate: 19.1 g
- Cholesterol: 0 mg
- Total Fat: 3.1 g
- Protein: 3.9 g
- Sodium: 265 mg

175. Zucchini And Tomato Casserole

"This dish is made of Romano cheese, tomato, and zucchini. It's light and tasty. You can adjust the recipe depending on your taste."
Serving: 8 | Prep: 15m | Ready in: 55m

Ingredients

- 4 zucchini, cubed
- 3 tablespoons chopped fresh dill weed
- ground black pepper to taste
- 1 tablespoon margarine, melted
- 2 large tomatoes, sliced
- 1 tablespoon chopped fresh basil leaves
- 3/4 cup grated Romano cheese

Direction

- Start preheating the oven to 350°F (175°C). Lightly oil a 2-quart casserole pan.
- Fit a steamer basket in a pot over boiling water and put zucchini. Steam until the zucchini is soft but not mushy, about 5 minutes. Move to the oiled casserole pan. Combine margarine, pepper, and dill, and mix into the casserole pan, evenly covering the zucchini. Put over the zucchini the tomato slices and use Romano cheese and basil to sprinkle.
- Put in the preheated oven and bake until it turns golden brown and bubbly, about 30 minutes.

Nutrition Information

- Calories: 80 calories;
- Total Carbohydrate: 5.7 g
- Cholesterol: 12 mg
- Total Fat: 4.6 g
- Protein: 5.2 g
- Sodium: 162 mg

Index

A

Almond, 18, 72

Apple, 4, 27, 31, 45, 54, 75, 88, 93, 96

Artichoke, 3, 12–13, 22

Asparagus, 73

Avocado, 4, 23, 51

B

Bacon, 3, 30, 39, 53–54, 57

Baking, 10–11, 14–15, 22, 25–27, 33, 38, 40, 44, 46–47, 52, 57, 68, 72, 76, 78, 80–83, 85, 90, 94

Baking powder, 25, 76, 78, 83, 85

Balsamic vinegar, 36, 79

Basil, 20, 59–60, 79–80, 92–93, 97

Bay leaf, 37, 59–61, 70, 91

Beans, 3–4, 10–11, 22, 41, 47, 49, 55, 63, 65, 76–77, 89, 92, 95

Beef, 3, 10–11, 15–16, 20, 33, 42–43, 50, 61, 89–91

Beef stock, 91

Berry, 5, 63, 97

Biscuits, 4, 13, 78

Black pepper, 9–10, 12–21, 23, 26–27, 30, 32–37, 39, 42, 45, 48–49, 51–52, 55–59, 61, 63–68, 70, 73–74, 76, 79–81, 83–84, 86, 88, 90–94, 96–97

Bread, 3–4, 11–13, 23, 26–27, 32–33, 35, 42–43, 51, 53–54, 56, 58, 61, 66–67, 76, 87, 90, 92, 96

Breadcrumbs, 26, 33, 68, 80, 82

Broccoli, 4, 21, 47, 62, 72, 95–96

Broth, 15–16, 18–19, 22, 24–25, 33, 42, 48, 54–55, 60–62, 70–71, 73, 90, 96

Brown rice, 4, 73

Brown sugar, 15, 64

Brussels sprouts, 3, 18

Buckwheat, 3, 16

Burger, 4, 50, 54

Butter, 3, 7, 10–11, 13–16, 18, 20, 25, 27, 33, 35, 44, 50–51, 54, 58, 64, 66–68, 77–78, 81–86

Butterhead lettuce, 87

Buttermilk, 29, 34, 62, 74, 78, 83, 85

Butternut squash, 18

C

Cabbage, 3–5, 18, 21, 54–55, 61, 66, 90–91

Cake, 4, 10, 20, 74, 78

Cannellini beans, 55

Capers, 63, 77, 80, 84, 86–87, 94

Carrot, 3–4, 13–14, 18–21, 23, 35, 44, 47–48, 59–60, 64, 70, 90–91, 96

Cauliflower, 3, 17, 21, 24–25, 47

Cayenne pepper, 13–14, 25, 34, 40, 66, 86, 93, 96

Celery, 9, 13, 17, 23–26, 35, 43–44, 48–49, 51, 58–60, 63–64, 70, 80, 88–89, 91, 95–96

Champagne, 22, 92

Chanterelle mushrooms, 19

Cheddar, 15–16, 42, 55, 66–67, 93

Cheese, 3–5, 7, 9–12, 15–16, 20–21, 27–29, 32, 36–37, 39–40, 42, 44, 47, 55–58, 66–67, 70, 72, 78–79, 82–83, 86, 93, 97

Cheese sauce, 9

Cherry, 67

Cherry tomatoes, 67

Chicken, 3–4, 12–16, 18–22, 24, 26, 33, 37–38, 48, 52–53, 55–56, 59–60, 62, 67, 72, 74, 77, 90, 92, 96

Chicken breast, 22, 26, 52, 56, 62

Chicken soup, 4, 59–60

Chicken stock, 13–14, 19, 37–38, 92

Chickpea, 3, 5, 23, 89

Chips, 28, 36, 55, 77, 87

Chives, 19, 22, 25, 29, 47, 55, 57, 67, 70–71, 87, 90, 95

Chopped tomatoes, 32

Chorizo, 3, 26

Cider, 27, 30–31, 37, 44–45, 52, 75, 88, 96

Clementine, 63–64

Cloves, 10, 12–13, 15, 17–18, 20, 23, 30, 37, 39–41, 46, 52, 55–56, 62, 68, 70–72, 75–76, 88–89, 91–92

Cod, 4, 67–68

Coriander, 68, 92

Corned beef, 43

Cottage cheese, 11, 58

Courgette, 31

Couscous, 69

Crab, 3, 26

Crackers, 28, 36, 39, 55, 77, 86

Cranberry, 63–64

Cranberry sauce, 63–64

Cream, 3, 5, 9, 13–14, 17–18, 20–21, 27–29, 31–33, 35–37, 39–40, 42–43, 48, 53, 57, 64–66, 70–71, 74, 77–82, 86–91

Cream cheese, 3, 5, 9, 20–21, 28–29, 36, 39, 70, 78–79, 82, 86

Crumble, 3, 11, 39, 80

Cucumber, 3–5, 9, 17, 21, 23–25, 27, 30, 32–33, 35–37, 45–46, 48, 56, 58, 64–65, 67, 71, 75, 87–88, 90

Cumin, 16–17, 48, 52, 58–60, 92

Curry, 30, 52, 60

Curry powder, 30, 52, 60

D

Dab, 85

Dijon mustard, 20, 22, 48–49, 70, 73, 76–77, 80, 88, 92–94, 97

Dill, 1, 3–7, 9–97

Dried fruit, 84

E

Egg, 3–5, 10–11, 15, 20–21, 25, 30–31, 33–34, 39, 44, 53, 59–60, 66–67, 72–73, 76, 78, 80, 82–86, 88, 90

Egg white, 39, 82, 84

Egg yolk, 34, 44, 66–67, 82, 84

English muffin, 86

F

Falafel, 5, 92

Fat, 9–98

Fennel, 4, 69

Feta, 3–4, 10, 12, 16, 21, 39, 47, 55–56

Fettuccine, 10–11

Fish, 4, 9, 12, 14–15, 30, 38, 40, 47, 50, 57, 67–71, 73, 79, 81, 83–85, 87

Fish sauce, 30

Flatbread, 4, 74

Flour, 10–11, 15–16, 20–22, 25, 31, 33–34, 42, 44, 62, 65, 72, 74, 76–78, 82–83, 85

French bread, 51

Fruit, 6, 42, 84

Fusilli, 95

G

Garlic, 3–4, 10–13, 15–21, 23–24, 28, 30–32, 34, 37, 39–41, 45–52, 54–57, 60–68, 70–76, 80–81, 88–93, 96

Gherkin, 46

Ginger, 18, 30, 48

Gouda, 20–21

Grain, 9, 96

Gravy, 42

Green beans, 3–4, 41, 49, 63, 76–77

Green cabbage, 18

Ground ginger, 30

H

Halibut, 3–4, 14, 70–71

Heart, 22, 93, 95–96

Herbs, 3–4, 13, 19, 22–25, 47, 57–59, 64, 67–68, 74, 76, 78, 84, 87, 93–94

Hollandaise sauce, 3, 44, 86

Honey, 15, 39, 67–68, 73

Horseradish, 5, 29, 87, 91

J

Jelly, 51

K

Ketchup, 50

Kidney, 89

Kidney beans, 89

Kohlrabi, 4, 59

L

Lamb, 4, 61

Leek, 10, 61

Lemon, 3–5, 10–14, 17, 19–20, 23–24, 28–29, 32, 35–36, 39–40, 43–45, 47–49, 51–57, 62–63, 65–68, 70–71, 73–74, 77–81, 83–84, 86–87, 89–91, 96–97

Lemon juice, 10–14, 17, 19–20, 23–24, 28–29, 32, 35–36, 39–40, 43–45, 47–49, 54–57, 62, 65–68, 70–71, 73–74, 78–81, 83, 87, 89–91, 96–97

Lettuce, 23, 53–54, 80, 84, 87, 93

Lime, 16–17, 20, 35, 83–84

Lime juice, 16–17, 20, 35, 83–84

M

Macaroni, 32

Margarine, 14, 97

Marrow, 91

Matzo, 4, 59–60

Mayonnaise, 7, 9, 13–14, 17, 20–21, 23, 26, 28–29, 34–36, 38–40, 43, 45, 48–49, 51, 53–54, 57, 62–63, 66, 72, 74, 79–80, 83–84, 88, 91, 94–96

Meat, 6, 14, 31, 60, 84, 89, 91

Melon, 12

Mesclun, 84

Milk, 9–10, 15, 19, 28–29, 32, 34, 42, 76, 82–83, 85, 94, 96

Mince, 50

Mint, 13, 16, 23–24, 47–49, 55, 61, 64

Mozzarella, 39–40

Muffins, 3, 25, 79, 85–86

Mushroom, 3–4, 18–21, 30, 61, 66–69, 89

Mustard, 4, 10–11, 13, 15, 20, 22, 30–31, 34, 37, 39, 41, 44, 48–51, 60, 70–71, 73, 76–77, 79–80, 83–84, 88, 91–97

Mustard powder, 30, 60

Mustard seeds, 31, 37

N

New potatoes, 4, 40, 50

Noodles, 42

Nori, 23

Nut, 26

O

Oil, 10, 12–13, 15–22, 24–27, 30–32, 34–36, 38, 40, 43–46, 48, 50–54, 56–63, 65–71, 74, 76–82, 89–93, 97

Olive, 4, 10, 12, 15–22, 24, 26–27, 32, 36, 38, 40, 43, 45, 48, 50–54, 56, 58–59, 61–63, 65–69, 74, 76–81, 89–90, 92–93, 95–97

Olive oil, 10, 12, 15–22, 24, 26–27, 32, 36, 38, 40, 43, 45, 48, 50–54, 56, 58–59, 61–63, 65–69, 74, 76–81, 89–90, 92–93, 97

Onion, 9–24, 26–28, 30–31, 33–37, 40, 42–45, 48–49, 51, 53–66, 68–70, 72, 74, 77, 80, 83–86, 88–97

Oregano, 20, 56, 76, 79–80

P

Papaya, 94

Paprika, 19, 34, 39, 57, 60, 77, 91

Parmesan, 5, 10, 15–16, 27, 39–40, 42, 44, 57, 83

Parsley, 10, 13–14, 19, 29–30, 36, 47–49, 53, 55, 57–60, 63–64, 66–68, 70–71, 74, 84, 87, 90, 92–96

Pasta, 3–5, 32, 48, 55, 67, 70, 90, 94–96

Pastry, 4, 72, 83, 85

Pasty, 74

Peas, 3–5, 12, 22, 47, 59, 68–69, 91, 97

Pecan, 93

Peel, 46–47, 52, 76, 85

Penne, 70

Pepper, 4–5, 9–52, 54–74, 76–84, 86–94, 96–97

Peppercorn, 15, 20, 31, 38, 70, 75, 91

Perch, 68

Pesto, 90

Pickle, 3–5, 31, 34, 36–37, 46, 50, 71, 75, 88, 94–96

Pie, 3–4, 10, 27, 72

Pine nut, 26

Plum, 21

Pork, 33

Port, 77

Potato, 3–5, 12–13, 23, 25, 28, 38, 43–45, 50, 57, 61, 77, 88, 92–93

Poultry, 83, 93

Puff pastry, 4, 72

Pulse, 23, 50, 52, 55, 74, 77–78

Q

Quinoa, 4, 74

R

Radish, 5, 47, 97

Rainbow trout, 47

Raisins, 24, 64

Red cabbage, 21

Red onion, 9, 16–17, 21, 30, 34, 54, 56, 69, 77, 85, 92

Red wine, 7, 9, 18, 20–21, 30, 43, 76–77

Red wine vinegar, 9, 18, 21, 43, 76–77

Rice, 3–4, 9, 16, 19, 22, 37, 53, 67, 73, 79, 90, 93

Rice vinegar, 93

Rose wine, 69

Rosemary, 20, 74, 76

Rye bread, 43

S

Safflower oil, 43

Sage, 18

Salad, 3–5, 9, 13, 16–17, 21–23, 26–27, 30, 32–33, 35, 42–43, 45, 48–49, 51, 56, 58, 62, 65, 67, 71, 80, 82, 84–85, 87–88, 90–97

Salmon, 3–5, 9, 15, 37–39, 47, 50–51, 53–54, 63, 67–70, 73, 77–82, 84–86

Salsa, 4, 69

Salt, 4, 9–12, 14–83, 85–94, 96–97

Sausage, 18, 26, 54

Savory, 5, 20, 25, 50, 54, 83

Savoy cabbage, 91

Sea salt, 70, 75, 80–81

Seafood, 26, 81

Seasoning, 4, 11–12, 28, 34, 36, 43, 46, 57, 59–61, 66, 87

Seaweed, 23

Seeds, 31, 37, 52, 58–59, 92

Semolina, 10

Sesame seeds, 92

Shallot, 32, 48, 70–71, 73–74, 81

Sherry, 52

Sherry vinegar, 52

Sirloin, 89

Smoked salmon, 4–5, 70, 77–79, 82, 85–86

Smoked trout, 5, 87

Soda, 11, 25, 76, 78

Sorrel, 3, 13

Soup, 3–5, 10–11, 13–14, 18–19, 23–25, 52–55, 59–60, 63, 73, 77, 89–91

Soy sauce, 19, 38

Spices, 6, 37, 49, 57, 74

Spinach, 3, 5, 10, 53, 61, 67, 84, 89

Spring onion, 31, 68

Squash, 3, 18, 24, 52

Steak, 3, 42, 70

Stock, 13–14, 19, 37–38, 66, 81, 90–93

Sugar, 3, 9–11, 13, 15, 17–18, 22–23, 25, 29–30, 33, 35, 37, 41–42, 45, 47, 49, 56, 59, 62–65, 69, 71, 75–78, 82–83, 85, 87–88, 91, 93–94, 96–97

Sweet potato, 3, 38

T

Tabasco, 18

Tahini, 92

Tarragon, 3, 22, 39–40, 55, 68, 70–71, 84–85, 93–94

Tea, 32

Thyme, 18, 20, 60, 70, 76, 78–80

Tilapia, 4, 57

Tofu, 3, 30

Tomato, 3–5, 10–12, 16, 21–23, 27, 30, 32, 36, 43, 48–49, 52–54, 56, 61, 67–69, 89–92, 94–97

Tomato juice, 10

Trout, 5, 47, 87

Turkey, 4, 63–64

Turkey breast, 4, 63–64

Turmeric, 22, 48, 63–64

V

Veal, 33

Vegan, 3, 5, 23, 31, 38, 74, 95–96

Vegetable oil, 15, 19–20, 26, 30–31, 34–35, 44, 58–61, 91–93

Vegetable stock, 66

Vegetables, 6, 9, 17–18, 22, 25, 27–28, 34, 44, 47, 49, 56, 59–61, 69, 74, 91

Vegetarian, 4, 23, 73–74

Vinegar, 9, 16–18, 21–23, 27, 30–37, 39–41, 43–46, 49, 52, 58, 69–71, 75–77, 79, 86, 88, 92–93, 96

W

Walnut, 5, 43, 48–49, 64, 96

Walnut oil, 43

Watercress, 87

White bread, 42

White pepper, 77

White sugar, 9–11, 15, 17, 25, 30, 33, 35, 41, 45, 63, 65, 71, 76, 83, 88, 91, 93, 97

White wine, 73, 81, 93

Wild rice, 3, 19, 79

Wine, 7, 9, 16, 18, 20–22, 30, 43, 69–70, 73, 76–77, 81, 92–93

Worcestershire sauce, 26, 34, 38, 54, 86, 93

Wraps, 3, 30

Y

Yeast, 11, 15, 42

Z

Zest, 32, 45, 52–54, 67, 70, 77–78, 86

Conclusion

Thank you again for downloading this book!

I hope you enjoyed reading about my book!

If you enjoyed this book, please take the time to share your thoughts and post a review on Amazon. It'd be greatly appreciated!

Write me an honest review about the book – I truly value your opinion and thoughts and I will incorporate them into my next book, which is already underway.

Thank you!

If you have any questions, **feel free to contact at:** msingredient@mrandmscooking.com

Ms. Ingredient

www.MrandMsCooking.com

Your Note

Your Note